GRAHAM

GRAHAM:
A Day in
Billy's
Life

Gerald S. Strober

DOUBLEDAY & COMPANY, INC., GARDEN CITY, NEW YORK, 1976

Photos by Russ Busby and Gerald S. Strober

ISBN: 0-385-11373-0
Library of Congress Catalog Card Number 75–40745
Copyright © 1976 by Gerald S. Strober

For Robin, Jonathan, and Lori

This book is based on a composite rather than a "typical" day in Billy Graham's life. In a genuine sense, there are few normal days in the evangelist's busy and complex schedule.

While he is able to spend some time each year at home in North Carolina, more often than not Mr. Graham is on the road, either presiding over a Crusade, fulfilling a speaking engagement or attending to the diverse interests of his world-wide evangelistic organization.

The reader will find Billy Graham at home, at a Crusade in Jackson, Mississippi, and on a personal visit to Israel.

It was my good fortune to be at the evangelist's side during the periods described in this book, and I am greatly indebted to him for his co-operation and helpful attitude. I am also grateful for assistance rendered by several members of the Billy Graham Evangelistic Association, especially Drs. T. W. Wilson, Grady Wilson and Walter Smyth. Other associates of Graham, including Don Bailey, George Wilson, Stephanie Wills and Charles Riggs, facilitated my research and impressed me with their unfailing courtesy and friendliness.

The preparation of this book was also aided by Marie Rodell, whose sudden passing was an immense blow from which her many friends and colleagues are still trying to recover.

All individuals mentioned in this book are real. The people associated with the Crusade are mentioned by their real names. Other names have been changed to protect the privacy of the individual.

—Gerald S. Strober

CONTENTS

INTRODUCTION

It always comes as a surprise to me when a gifted writer and interpreter of our faith wishes to tell something about me. "The day" is one of many similar ones. If anything has been omitted in this book it is the larger one of the activities of members of my Team, members of local Crusade committees and, most of all, of the sacrifice my own wife and children have made because of my ministry.

I could wish that no one reading this record would fail to see the beautiful manifestation of the power and sovereignty of God in this Crusade ministry. As for me, I can claim no supernatural power of my own. There are many godly and talented men, but God has chosen me in his sovereign right to proclaim the message of salvation through faith in his son Jesus Christ. Now this is a humbling truth. Therefore I find myself in the position of John and Charles

Wesley, who took as a guiding passage from the Psalms, "Not unto us, O Lord, not unto us, but unto thy name give glory, for thy mercy and for thy truth's sake" (Psalm 115:1).

—Billy Graham

February 20, 1976

CHAPTER 1   MORNING

It is just after seven o'clock on a warm and sunny spring morning and Jackson, Mississippi, the capital of the Deep South and the cradle of the Confederacy, is coming alive. Out at the Municipal airport the first Eastern jet is rolling down the runway on its way to Atlanta, and a few miles farther south Bill C. Franklin is delivering mail on his suburban route. Closer to downtown, in the old, tree-lined, residential section of town, Dr. Philip Pollner, a transplanted New Yorker, is putting his frayed medical bag in the trunk of a small foreign car and making the last preparations for the eighty-mile drive to the clinic he helped establish in the Delta crossroads of Dixonville. At his modern ranch house on Roebuck Drive, Tom Bailey is finishing the first cup of coffee of the day and placing some papers in order before he drives to his job as vice president of the Mississippi State Bank, and in a nearby shopping center Sarah Herndon is ringing up some items at a supermarket check-out counter. The cooks at Morrison's cafeteria are busy with the normal breakfast traffic, and at police headquarters the day shift officers are moving toward their patrol cars and motorcycles. Jimmy and Carol Wheatly are running, as they usually do, to catch the bus that will take them to Parkside Junior High School, and in the intensive care unit of the University Medical Center, Linda May Rogers is carefully monitoring the breathing of an Ellis Avenue insurance salesman who suffered a heart attack during the night.

An early-morning meditation

At the Holiday Inn North on Frontage Road, a middle-aged man on his first visit to Jackson in twenty-three years munches on a piece of toast and watches the "Today" show news report from his top floor suite. There are many things this visitor could do on this lovely morning; he could drive the seven miles to downtown and tour the state capitol, or he might head for the museum to view the artifacts of the pre-bellum South, or, if he has brought his fishing gear, he could stop along the Ross Barnett Reservoir to see if the catfish and walleyes are in a biting mood, but he will not have the time to attempt any of these pleasant diversions. In a few minutes he will sit at the bedroom desk and read from a well-thumbed copy of the Living Bible; and then, the day's portion of scripture perused and absorbed, he will bow his head and he will meditate upon the many concerns that are on his heart and the multitude of questions that have been put to him for advice and decision; and he will especially remember why he has left the beautiful mountain country of western North Carolina to come to this city; and he will think of all the tasks and responsibilities that await him this day; and he will be humbled and finally, as he does each day of his life, he will ask God for strength, wisdom and blessing upon his ministry.

As Billy Graham studies and prays, the switchboard in his Minneapolis headquarters is beginning to light up with the first of the hundreds of long-distance calls that will come in during the day, a secretary in his Paris office types a letter to an Antwerp clergyman who has requested a meeting with the evangelist during his upcoming trip to Belgium, and a Tokyo-based representative of the Billy Graham Evangelistic Association is holding a working luncheon in Taipei with the committee planning an island-wide series of meetings for the late fall. Back in Jackson, members of the Graham Team who have gathered in the city to aid in the Greater Mississippi Crusade are converging on the National Guard Armory where the 7th Annual Governor's Prayer Breakfast will be held.

The Wilson brothers

At five minutes to eight, T. W. Wilson, a solidly built, balding, ordained minister who is one of Billy's oldest and closest friends and who since 1963 has served as Graham's personal chief of staff and traveling companion, comes into the small bedroom and hands Billy the morning paper. "Grady is waiting downstairs for us," Wilson says. "We've got to be out to the armory in fifteen minutes." Graham finishes dressing, he knots a light blue tie and puts on a maroon-colored sports jacket.

The lobby of the hotel is crowded with representatives of a local manufacturing firm who are conducting a sales conference, and as he leaves the elevator he is quickly spotted. A wave of excitement sweeps over the room, fingers point, hands are outstretched, a sudden rush of sound blots out the inane hum of the omnipresent piped-in music. T.W. skillfully propels Billy through the crush of people, and in a few moments T.W.'s brother, Grady, has maneuvered a blue and white Pontiac sedan out onto North State Street.

Grady turns around to greet Billy; he is a heavy-set, red-faced, highly intelligent, friendly man and a great storyteller.

Grady and T.W. made decisions for Christ at the same series of meetings that brought about Billy Graham's conversion, and the three men have been very close for over forty years. Grady was one of the original members of the

Graham Team, and while he now conducts his own evangelistic meetings, he is never far from Billy during a Crusade or on many of Billy's other speaking engagements and foreign journeys. Grady can make Billy relax and he can always crack Billy up with a story from the old days.

This morning as Billy goes over the notes for his prayer breakfast talk Grady reminisces about his first sermon, which was preached at the Sixteenth Street Rescue Mission in their hometown of Charlotte, North Carolina. Grady's topic was "God's Four Questions," and he spent one and a half hours on the first question. "I can still see Billy and his date squirming, wondering if I'd ever finish. Well, I did," Grady says, "but by that time everyone else was asleep!" Although he has likely heard this story a thousand times before, Billy laughs and then asks T.W. about the remainder of the day's schedule.

The day's schedule

Wilson hands Billy a typewritten sheet with the following information:

8:30	Governor's Prayer Breakfast
11:00	Address to School of Evangelism
12:00	Tour of Crusade Office
2:00	Staff Conferences
6:00	Departure for Stadium
7:30	Crusade Meeting
10:00	Dinner at the Home of Crusade Chairman, James Carr

Wilson also reminds Billy that Johnny Cash, his wife, June Carter, and the Cash aggregation are flying in later in the day to appear at tonight's meeting. Unfortunately Johnny, who is a close personal friend of Billy's, cannot stay over but must return to Nashville immediately after the service to keep an early morning recording date.

The schedule Billy studies lists only official functions and appointments and is not a comprehensive projection of what

Graham's day will be like. Other appointments and meetings will be added, there will be telephone calls to make and receive, unexpected special visitors, correspondence to be read and answered and perhaps an unanticipated crisis or two. In addition, Billy will need to spend at least two hours alone in the afternoon going over his Crusade message, which tonight will be taped for later national TV distribution.

This is the fourth day of an eight-day Crusade and during the first three days Billy has already held a press conference, given a reception for local Crusade leaders, addressed a ministers' meeting, attended the Team breakfast, appeared on three television programs, visited the offices of the advertising agency that is handling his Jackson public relations and toured the campus of a Presbyterian seminary that has recently dedicated a new building in memory of his late father-in-law, Dr. L. Nelson Bell.

1,850 guests for breakfast

The National Guard Armory is filled to capacity when we arrive, and a buzz of noise emanates from the massive hall as Billy enters from a side door and is recognized. His immense charisma is obvious, every eye in the room is focused upon him, every conversation includes his name.

Governor Bill Waller, a kind of later-day populist who confounded the political experts by his upset win in the last election, gets up from his place at the dais to greet Graham. Waller, whose wife has known Grady Wilson from school days in Charlotte, is genuinely pleased to have the famous evangelist highlight his prayer breakfast. He introduces Billy and notes that Graham represents those "Christian principles which many kinds of people can agree upon."

"We have the honor," he continues, "of welcoming the world's greatest evangelist to Mississippi, and on behalf of two and a half million God-fearing Mississippians, we welcome you to the Magnolia State, the friendliest state in the union. We hope that your stay here will be one of the friendliest, warmest and, we hope, the most spiritual visit that you've ever made to any part of the world."

In a thinly veiled reference to the racial question, an issue which has special pertinence in Jackson, long considered the last bastion of opposition to legislative- and court-enforced integration, Waller calls Graham "a symbol of the fact that people can get together for worship without obstacles or barriers; he gives people a chance to realize that with God there are no barriers."

Later in the morning Waller, who has had Graham to lunch at the executive mansion two days previously, tells me how impressed he is by Graham's grasp of current issues. They had spent a happy hour or so discussing politics, and Waller marveled at how relaxed Graham appeared in spite of his heavy schedule. The governor also tells me that he and his wife "support Billy with our money and our prayers," and I tend to believe him because, in the first place, I am not a constituent he needs to impress and, secondly, he cannot constitutionally seek another term as governor.

In his speech to the 1,850 breakfast guests, Graham suggests that the credibility of the United States has been weakened by recent events. In the immediate post-Watergate era no one in the room has to ask what these events might be. The evangelist maintains that this credibility gap has the whole world watching the United States to determine if the nation will continue to live up to her commitments.

Graham adds that 1976, the year of the Bicentennial observance, needs to be launched on a "spiritual basis," receives a standing ovation and is quickly ushered out to the parking area where Grady already has the Pontiac's engine running.

It is now nine-thirty and there are a number of matters related to the operation of the Billy Graham Evangelistic Association (BGEA) awaiting his immediate attention. T.W. accompanies Graham to his hotel suite, while Grady heads for the School of Evangelism to check out arrangements for Billy's late-morning appearance.

Organization of a Crusade

When Billy re-enters his suite, Stephanie Wills, his bright and highly efficient secretary, is waiting with a batch of letters brought down from Minneapolis the night before by Sherwood Wirt, editor of *Decision* magazine. Woody, as he is affectionately known in the Graham organization, is in Jackson to oversee the magazine's coverage of the Crusade. Billy looks over the mail and separates out some letters that he will answer during the next hour. The phone rings and Stephanie tells Graham that Jim Carr, the chairman of the Crusade Executive Committee, is calling to remind him of the dinner at the Carrs' home later this evening. T.W. remarks that Carr is a very persistent and persevering man. I ask T.W. what he means, and T.W. tells me something of the genesis of the Jackson Crusade.

About five years before when Carr was president of the local Jaycees, the organization passed a resolution inviting Billy Graham to come to Jackson. At almost the same time a group of ministers were working to influence Graham to hold a Crusade in town. The lay and clergy groups met together and formed an ad hoc committee, which circulated a petition among the churches asking Graham to come to the city.

Carr was named to head the ad hoc committee, and he met with Grady Wilson when the latter came to Jackson for an Easter sunrise service. Wilson told Carr that Billy would consider an invitation only if it was broad-based and reflected the sentiment of the majority of the local churches. He also advised Carr that the process of invitation was detailed and demanding, and in the light of the fact that twenty cities were then seriously in contention for major Crusades, it might be some time before Jackson could be put on the Crusade schedule.

Carr, who is a successful businessman and a devout believer, was determined to see the project through and he was fortunate to have the support of his wife, Martha, who realized there would be endless meetings, phone calls and frustrations involved in developing a Crusade.

Several months after Wilson's visit to Jackson, Carr and four colleagues from the ad hoc committee flew to Birmingham, Alabama, where Graham was conducting a Crusade. The afternoon they arrived they met with key Graham associates including Grady and Cliff Barrows. The committee members brought along a book of letters from state and city officials and local civic and religious leaders. They also presented information provided by the Chamber of Commerce on the economic and social structure of Jackson and on the facilities available for a major Crusade. Grady and Cliff were impressed enough to ask the delegation to stay overnight so they could meet with Graham. That night the Jackson group spent a few moments with the evangelist just prior to the service, and he promised that Jackson would be given careful consideration. Most of the committee members went back to Jackson expecting to hear that Graham would come within the year, but Carr knew that this was only the beginning. For the next two years he kept the committee alive and would not allow himself the luxury of discouragement, although he now admits that there were times when he doubted that a Crusade would ever take place in Jackson.

During this period the ad hoc committee was in contact with Walter Smyth, then head of Crusades for the Graham organization, and Smyth told the group that Jackson was on the list but there was as yet no definite commitment as to dates.

In the fall of 1974, Sterling Huston, now in charge of Graham's North American schedule, came to Jackson and met with the committee and with a larger group of local leadership. Two months later, almost four years after the original Jaycee resolution had been passed, Sterling telephoned Jim Carr and told him that Mr. Graham would like to come to Jackson in May 1975.

At this point the ad hoc committee was formalized into a Crusade committee and Carr was elected chairman. The Graham organization, which relies heavily on local participation for a viable Crusade, prefers to have a lay person head the Crusade. They require, as Sterling Huston says, "a successful businessman who is used to getting the job done," and Carr, whose dogged determination was a matter of record, certainly fit the bill. The Crusade Committee was also led by three vice-chairmen, each a minister representing the community's major denominations, in this case, Baptist, Methodist and Presbyterian. The chairman and vice-chairman along with twenty other persons made up the Executive Committee. The group was then divided into subcommittees responsible for prayer, women's work, youth activities, finance, ushers, counseling and follow-up. The Executive Committee then drew up a budget for the Crusade. Budgets, which in all cases are based on actual costs, differ from city to city. Normally the most significant single item is the auditorium or stadium rental. In some cases the Crusade will be given free use of a site; in other situations the rental fee is quite steep. In the 1969 New York City Crusade the local committee paid $22,000 a night for the use of Madison Square Garden. Here in Jackson the 46,000-seat football stadium will be available at a relatively nominal cost.

Budget of a Crusade

The Crusade budget, which eventually is fixed at $266,000, will be raised in several ways. The Finance Committee will work closely with the Graham organization to develop a complement of "Share Partners," individuals who will donate a fixed sum for the operation of the Crusade. Usually the funds from the Share Partners will pay the pre-Crusade costs. Share Partners are obtained through a letter that goes out to all persons on the *Decision* magazine mailing list who live within a fifty-mile radius of Jackson.

In the case of the Jackson Crusade this letter produced about two thousand positive responses. Finance Committee members also conducted individual solicitations for funds, and about one third of the budget was raised through these personal contacts. The remainder of the budget came from offerings taken at each Crusade session.

Once the Administrative Committee has been organized

and the budget fixed, the Graham organization sends in a specialist who will direct the over-all Crusade operation. The Crusade director serves as a liaison between the Billy Graham Evangelistic Association and the local sponsoring committee. The local committee makes all the decisions involving the conduct of the Crusade; the Graham associate is responsible for the execution of these decisions.

The Jackson group was favored by the services of Charles Riggs, a seasoned veteran of countless big-city Crusades and an organizing genius of the first rank. As Jim Carr says, "When I heard that Charlie Riggs was being assigned to Jackson, I knew everything was going to be all right."

Riggs, a tall, raw-boned, graying native of Texas, has been with Graham since 1953. Before that he worked with the Navigators, an evangelistic group which carries on an aggressive scripture memorization ministry among the armed services.

In January of 1975 Charlie and his wife left their Nashville home and took an apartment in Jackson. An office with about three thousand square feet of working space was secured adjacent to the stadium. The office became the hub of Crusade activity for a four-month period; hundreds of volunteers will stuff envelopes, prepare lists and perform the many nuts-and-bolts chores involved in putting a Crusade together. There will also be a paid staff of ten people including a bookkeeper, secretaries and skilled mailing clerks.

Under Riggs's direction the Jackson metropolitan area will be broken down into ten geographic areas. Each area will have a chairman for men, women, youth and pastors. These chairmen, who provide the Crusade with four lines into the local church, will complete a three-week Bible-study course and they will be given a thorough orientation concerning the various aspects of the Crusade operation. The area chairmen will in turn identify and train two more echelons of workers, persons representing each of the zip codes in their area and representatives from each of the area's churches.

These people are then channeled into a prayer program that will eventually involve sixty thousand local people meeting each day to pray for the Crusade's success. Once the prayer groups are set in motion, Riggs meets with the pastors in each area. He shares Crusade plans and indicates how they can participate. He also tells them what the Crusade can do for the local church. The ministers are asked to recruit their congregants for assignments as counselors, ushers and choir members. Riggs also urges the pastors to bring busloads of people to the Crusade sessions.

"Operation Andrew"

This aspect of the Crusade is known as "Operation Andrew" and in Jackson will account for an average of twenty-two thousand reservations a night, an important attendance base when you are trying to fill up a forty-six-thousand-seat stadium. In the Dallas-Fort Worth Crusade "Operation Andrew" brought in thirty-five to forty thousand people to each service.

The Crusade Committee's intensive organizing effort mobilized a significant portion of the church community and led Jim Carr to remark that "even if for some reason the Graham people had at the last minute to cancel out, it would have been worth it. People joined together in Bible study, prayer and got to know each other."

Four weeks before the first Crusade service, Cliff Barrows flew in for a workers' rally at the Calvary Baptist Church. At about the same time a special men's breakfast was held in the First Baptist Church with Dallas Cowboys' coach, Tom Landry, as the featured speaker. Up to this point most of the organizational activity was internal in nature, the persons thus far involved would all play a role in the Crusade. Once the workers were identified, trained and fired with enthusiasm the Crusade Committee turned its attention to the general public, and billboard and bus advertisements along with twice-daily radio programs began to inform the population that Billy Graham would soon be in town. An air of excitement pervaded the city, and by the time I arrived in Jackson four days before the start of the Crusade, Billy Graham seemed to be the name on everyone's lips.

Back at the suite in the Holiday Inn, Graham is in the middle of dictating a note to Stephanie Wills when Cliff Barrows walks into the room.

He is one of the original members of the Team; he and his wife, Billie, traveled with Billy, Grady and George Beverly Shea in the early post-World War II days, and thirty years of close association with Graham have not at all dulled his appreciation and respect for the man.

Cliff is smiling; he is by nature a deeply satisfied and happy person. He tells Billy that the TV tape of the previous evening's service looks very good and will require little editing. Although Cliff is best known as the Crusade music director and emcee, he also serves as Graham's radio- and television-program director. Each morning after a service is taped for possible television usage, Cliff studies the film and determines how much of the material can be processed for national distribution. Cliff also is responsible for the "Hour of Decision" radio broadcast, and this vital chore, along with his recording dates and personal appearance schedules, keeps him very busy.

Cliff Barrows

An ordained Baptist minister, Cliff served as assistant pastor of St. Paul's Temple Baptist Church back in the mid-forties and he is an outstanding speaker. He would have been satisfied to pursue a career in the ministry, but he feels that God called him to work with Graham. Indeed, his relationship to the evangelist has given Barrows a far greater opportunity to preach to diverse and large audiences than he ever could have hoped for as a pastor of a local congregation.

Cliff tells Billy he will see him at the School of Evangelism, and I ask if I can ride with him over to the First Baptist Church. I am interested in viewing Graham through Cliff's eyes and I ask Barrows how he accounts for Billy's success. "His simplicity, sincerity and integrity are the three primary reasons for his success," Cliff responds. "This is why God has opened so many doors for him. You have to remember that Billy has an absolute trust in the word of God. He has been a man of integrity and consistency in the proclamation of God's message." Barrows also talks of Graham's unique gifts. He recalls that even in the early days Billy had a keen interest in political affairs; he would read the news magazines; he would ask questions, seek out knowledgeable people; he had a breadth and depth that were unusual for that day.

I ask Cliff what it is like to be with Billy for long periods of time: is he temperamental? how does he treat his staff and associates? Cliff replies, "I've spent as much time with him as I have with my family; in a sense the Team is a family, and after thirty years he is as warm and friendly and as interested in people as he ever was." Cliff adds, "Many men along in years are content with what they have accomplished. I'm continually amazed at his interest in every aspect of the Kingdom of God."

I am interested in what Barrows has said about being

with Billy as much as his own wife and children—doesn't this cause a strain in familial relationships?—but he tells me that ever since his children were very little they understood that "Daddy has to be away with Billy Graham." One night his eight-year-old son prayed, "God save everybody so Daddy can stay home."

Barrows, like all of the key people around Graham, is convinced he is a part of a vital, even historic ministry, and this apparently enables him and his associates to make personal sacrifices that people in more mundane situations would not countenance.

School of Evangelism

We reach the First Baptist Church and I am handed a packet of materials that describe the School of Evangelism and its program. The initial paragraph of welcome reads:

> The Billy Graham Crusade School of Evangelism is designed to focus your attention on the dynamic of the Gospel. This supplement to seminary studies is designed to inspire pastors and key lay leaders to a greater emphasis on evangelistic activity together with tested methods for local church outreach. In this crisis hour of our nation's history the church is confronted with its greatest opportunity. The School is planned to enable the pastor to take maximum advantage of the times in which we live.
>
> We are here to enjoy five days of intellectually and spiritually exciting moments. Make new friends. Mutually share spiritual experiences. Discuss programs which are working in the field of evangelism. Be available to God. There are menial and exalted opportunities awaiting you. Be early to each meeting. Don't miss a word of an event. To this unique experience Billy Graham and his entire Team welcome you.

Later I learn more about the school and its mode of operation from the dean, Dr. Kenneth Chaffin. Chaffin has a distinguished academic and organizational background in the field of evangelism. He was Billy Graham Professor of Evangelism at Southern Baptist Theological Seminary and he headed the Department of Evangelism of the eleven-million-member Southern Baptist Convention. He is also the author of several books and hosts the syndicated TV series, "Spring Street U.S.A." Currently he is pastor of Houston's South Main Baptist Church, one of the largest congregations in the United States.

Chaffin, along with Harold Lindsell, the editor of *Christianity Today*, Sherwood Wirt, editor of *Decision* magazine and Dr. Robert D. Ferm represent the intellectual vanguard of the Graham movement. He describes the history of the School of Evangelism in didactic but enthusiastic terms.

The school owes its formation to Lowell Berry, a Presbyterian layman from San Francisco, who was active in the Oakland Crusade and came away convinced that theological students (he served on the board of a Bay Area seminary) were not being exposed to the evangelistic orientation manifested by Graham. He asked Billy to set up a school of evangelism for theological students in conjunction with his Crusades. Billy liked the idea, but he had many other matters on his mind when the proposal was first made and he did not initially react in a positive manner. Berry, however, was quite persistent, and finally after Graham said, "Well, Lowell, this is going to cost a lot of money," Berry responded that he was prepared to provide the necessary funding.

Today the schools are held at each Crusade with an annual budget exceeding $250,000. At first the student body consisted only of seminarians, but later pastors were included and finally lay people were invited to participate. One recent innovation has been the inclusion of wives in the activity of the school.

The students' lodging is paid for by the Graham organization, and they also receive a stipened to help with transportation. Since the Jackson Crusade is regional in nature the school will draw pupils from Mississippi, Alabama, Tennessee and Louisiana. The school runs from Monday through Friday and consists of a morning plenary, six or seven afternoon seminars and nightly attendance at the Crusade service.

While the school could be operative in different settings, Chaffin believes the "atmosphere of the Crusade creates an unbelievable context for learning." In Jackson the thirteen hundred registrants will hear Dr. Basil Jackson, a clinical psychiatrist on the faculty of the University of Wisconsin, Dr. Paul Little, author and assistant to the president of the Inter-Varsity Christian Fellowship, and Dr. Charles L. Allen, pastor of the eleven-thousand-member First United Methodist Church of Houston, in addition to Grady Wilson, Lindsell, Riggs and other Team members.

Why Jackson?

In my conversation with Chaffin I decide to ask a few tough questions. Why does Graham bother to come to Jackson, at best a medium-sized city and one which has a huge number of churches and presumably a very high density of evangelical Christians? Isn't this an easy ride for Graham and shouldn't he be out trying to reach the tougher Northern cities with their large unchurched populations.

Chaffin is soft spoken but very direct and unapologetic. He explains that the strategy in going to smaller cities revolves around the television aspect of the Graham ministry. Jackson, like Albuquerque, the first stop, and Lubbock, Texas, the next port of call on Graham's 1975 United States agenda, requires less preparation than a major metropolitan area and provides, either in an auditorium or medium-sized stadium setting, a TV studio from which the Crusade may be aired to all parts of the nation. By conducting Crusades in the Jacksons and Lubbocks, Graham can have more television opportunities than if he held fewer and of necessity longer lasting big-city Crusades.

Why, then, I asked, go to the trouble of coming to Jackson, why not just produce a program in a television studio?

Chaffin responds that you can never get the same effect and excitement in a studio, but more important than this,

Graham's appearance in places like Albuquerque, Jackson and Lubbock acts to revitalize and energize the churches and provides a vehicle for co-operation and united action that has long-lasting, positive impact. Chaffin's words bring to mind a discussion I had with Jim Carr, who told me of the "lifetime effect the Crusade had upon my life." Carr added, the Crusade, "made me realize what it means to be a Christian, it made me understand that though we live in the Bible Belt we still have a mission in our neighborhood."

"Anyway," Chaffin concludes, "Billy does go to some very difficult places, like Seoul, Korea, where he pulled over one million people to a service, and Baltimore, where he will hold a major Crusade in 1976."

I then ask Chaffin the question I am to pose to many of Graham's associates during the days I spend in Jackson: why is Graham so successful whether he is standing on evangelical turf or on relatively alien ground? Chaffin says that to answer the question fully one must seek to understand the success of evangelical Christianity itself.

"The emptiness of man and the adequacy of the gospel transcend the Moodys and the Billy Grahams. The gospel is unchanging and has survived as something much more attractive than the various alternatives which have caught the public's attention. I feel evangelicalism is just at the beginning of its best period in recent history. Liberal Christianity has pretty much struck out and evangelical Christianity has become a little more whole, more interested in a ministry to the total person."

As I stand near the book table looking at the titles on display, the sanctuary doors open and people begin to flow out into the hallway. The plenary has recess for a fifteen-minute break; when it resumes, Graham will speak.

I talk with a few of the students, and one, a thirty-year-old pastor from a rural Mississippi town, tells me how delighted he is to be at the School of Evangelism. "This is like a blood transfusion to me; you really can stagnate when you're out there away from the seminary, theological libraries and interaction with colleagues."

I wonder how effectively Graham will be able to communicate with this young man and the many other pastors and church workers who have come to Jackson from dozens of southern hamlets and way-stops. Can he possibly understand their problems and concerns, is he at all aware of the lives they lead, the issues that are important in their delta outposts? True, Graham grew up on a farm; the Charlotte of his day was a relatively small town, sheltered from the glitter and façade of sophistication offered by the large population centers. But Graham has come a long way from the Charlotte homestead, and his mind is preoccupied with the enormous problems involved with running a world-wide operation. I also wonder if his fame and notoriety will not intimidate his audience, or if there will not be a current of jealousy and envy even from the ministers of the Jackson churches. Will not some of them ask themselves why Graham has risen so far while they labor in the provinces?

Of course, the standard and expected answer to these queries would be that every Christian worker is happy in the context in which he has been placed by God, and, anyway, God cannot utilize too many Billy Grahams; there must be, after all, foot troops and rear-rank soldiers to carry out the routine tasks involved in the building of the Kingdom of God. Yet I am an outsider; I tend to operate on a less elevated plane than the spiritual level operative in the Crusade and I know that I would be very envious of Graham if I were the pastor of a Mississippi parish.

Speaking to clergymen

When Billy begins to speak, after a gracious introduction from Chaffin and another standing ovation, one part of my questions is answered: Graham can and does relate to his audience of clergymen. He has changed his shirt—this one is yellow and he now wears a blue-striped tie and he looks very relaxed and confident as he stands in the pulpit. He begins by stating he cannot speak for too long a period since he has come down with a slight virus. His throat is sore, and this reminds me of the story Grady told me earlier in the day of the other Jackson Crusade twenty-three years before. One day Grady and Cliff Barrows went on a fishing expedition and spent the night trading tall stories with some local ministers. When they returned to town the next afternoon they found Billy in his room with a high fever and unable to talk.

"Billy looked at me and said, 'You've got to preach tonight.'

"Well," Grady recalls, "I was tired and sunburned and had almost lost my voice but I was not about to tell him that."

The story is instructive as well as amusing. It provides an insight into how much more relaxed the Graham organization was twenty-odd years ago; as I watch Cliff and Grady this week in Jackson I don't see how they have time to go out for a sandwich and a cup of coffee, let alone go fishing.

Graham then tells the clergy that he had hoped to play some golf while in Jackson but the weather was not cooperating. He did go out to a country club with two or three members of the Crusade Executive Committee two days before, but the party was forced off the course by a rainstorm after five holes. Grady was out picking up some dry cleaning when the group left the hotel, and Billy put a note on his door telling him to come out to the club, but the older Wilson brother had decided to take the advice the famed golf professional Sam Snead had once offered: stop playing for two or three months and then give up the game completely.

Billy, who is always on the lookout for jokes or anecdotes to use in his messages, then told the story of the man whose wife was after him because he wasn't going to Sunday school. She said, "You know, there are three reasons why you should be in Sunday school every Sunday. One is that you had a godly mother who always insisted you go to Sunday school, and she'd be disappointed if you didn't go. The second reason is, you're now over forty years old and it's time you established good habits. And thirdly, you're pastor of the church!"

This broke the audience up and was followed up by two or three other stories. Graham then became serious and commented on the changes he had seen in Jackson since his earlier Crusade there.

"I commended you," he said, "for the way you have reacted to the tremendous social changes which have taken place in this state since we were here twenty-three years ago." And, as if in response to my question to Ken Chaffin, Graham continued. "Many people wondered why we came to Jackson when we could go to this city or that city that's larger than Jackson. I answered by saying that we came here to get something of the blessing and the thrill and the joy that we find here in Mississippi among both black and white people that I believe has made a contribution to our own Team, that's opened the eyes of some of our own Team members about Mississippi. And also I wanted to say something on the television about Mississippi to people in other parts of the country, which I was able to do."

As I listen to these words, I am tempted to think that is Graham pandering to his audience. Yet I know from conversations with him that he really believes the South, and even the Deep South, has advanced dramatically in terms of racial accord. As a Southerner, Graham often feels a sense of frustration and even outrage when he hears charges of recalcitrance on the racial question leveled against the region. To some degree this reaction is similar to the feelings expressed by his very close friend the late Lyndon Johnson when the former President heard the South maligned over the race problem.

W. F. Minor, Mississippi correspondent for the New Orleans *Times Picayune*, discussed this theme in a dispatch from Jackson. "When the idea of getting Graham back came up in local church circles nearly two years ago, it was learned that the evangelist would not deal with any group unless it had a totally biracial structure. This set in motion what some church leaders now are saying is a healthy new basis for interracial communication, which has been slow to come in certain church circles here."

Billy tells his audience that despite what he has heard concerning the economic problems of Mississippi, he has been impressed with the size of the Crusade offerings. "Either you love the Lord far more than any other place we have ever been and you give, or you may not be tithing to your church and you give it to us."

This remark drew another wave of laughter and applause, and when the audience settled down, Graham talked about the fellowship he had enjoyed with people representing many denominations. "You know," he said, "after a while you begin to see that God has his people everywhere."

"Co-operative Evangelism"

As his ministry has broadened, Graham has been criticized by evangelicalism's right wing for consorting with main-line denominational types and "liberals." One wonders what the reaction of these folk will be if Billy accepts a recent invitation to hold a Crusade on the campus of Notre Dame University. Years ago a book entitled *Cooperative Evangelism* outlined Graham's philosophy of inclusionism as it relates to Crusade sponsorship. Graham feels that evangelicals tend to be too exclusivistic in their outreach, thus limiting the scope and potential impact of their ministry. He has made a concerted effort to bring to a Crusade as wide a scope of community support as is possible, albeit within the context of a basic commitment to the doctrine of personal salvation through Christ. In a place as heavily saturated with evangelicals as Jackson, most of the churches who refuse to co-operate with the Crusade represent an extreme right-wing viewpoint, while the situation would be very different in a Boston, Chicago or New York, where opposition to his ministry would normally come from the more liberally oriented congregations. In spite of the problems emanating from either pole of American Protestantism, a typical Graham Crusade manages to win the support of about 80 per cent of the local churches, and this, along with encouragement engendered by civic groups, provides a very firm base for a successful operation.

An editorial in *The Baptist Record*, the official journal of the Mississippi Baptist Convention, dealt with the question of co-operation.

> As to compromise, if there has been any, it is that the liberals and non-evangelicals have compromised their position in cooperating with Billy Graham. Not for one moment has he ever compromised his position that the Bible is the inspired Word of God, or that every person is a sinner and must be born again through repentance between God and faith in the Lord Jesus Christ.

Graham next mentions that he and some associates including Charlie Riggs have recently been in Northeast India where they preached to audiences representing seventeen language groups.

"They told me there would be a sunrise service and I said, 'Oh, let Charlie take it,' then they said there will be a hundred thousand people there and I said, 'I think I'll take it!'"

Before he begins his actual sermon Graham thanks Ken Chaffin for his leadership and for being "a pastor to pastors." He also commends Dr. Pollard, the pastor of the First Baptist Church, for lending the excellent facilities and mentions Lowell Berry, who comes to each Crusade to observe the operation of the School of Evangelism.

The transition to the message is rather abrupt; he opens his Bible and says "I want to take a text that all of you have preached on many, many times, I Corinthians 1:17–18, 'for Christ sent me not to baptize but to preach the gospel, not with wisdom of words, lest the cross of Christ be made of none effect, for the preaching of the cross is to them as foolishness but unto us which are saved it is the power of God.'"

Graham's theme revolves around the problem of making the gospel relevant to modern man. He tells the pastors and church workers that they should expect their listeners to have emptiness, loneliness, guilt, the fear of death and a deep-seated insecurity "in their hearts." The gospel to be effective must be preached as a holy word with authority, simplicity, repetition and urgency. "It's not your logic or in-

tellectualism or your arguments, and it's not mine," the evangelist cautions his audience, "which works. There is something about the gospel that has its own power."

"The Bible says"

These comments do not suggest that Graham is either
anti-intellectual or irrational in his approach. He believes
the Bible has supernatural power and he fully expects people to respond to his message if he is faithful in articulating
the teaching of scripture. His sermons are replete with biblical references; perhaps the most common phrase of his
collected sermons would be "the Bible says." When he tells
his audience of church workers that the gospel "has its own
power" he is not dealing in theory but speaking out of a lifetime of personal experience and observation.

As an evangelist he understands his particular calling to
inform men of their sinfulness and their need to accept Jesus
as Lord and Savior. His task is to bring men to the point
where, in total submission to God, they recognize their utter
dependence upon Christ's work of redemption at the cross
and allow Jesus to come into their lives to bring salvation.

He constantly repeats "John 3:16—For God so loved the
world, he gave his only begotten son, that whosoever
believeth in him shall not perish but shall have everlasting
life; Romans 10:9—If thou shalt confess with thy mouth the
Lord Jesus and believe in thine heart that God hath raised
him from the dead, thou shalt be saved," and other classic
scriptural passages that summarize the process of salvation.
Once salvation has been accomplished the sinner becomes
transformed, he is a new person, he receives a new nature
and a new heart. One of Graham's favorite and most often
used verses of scripture describes this new birth—"If any
man be in Christ he is a new person, old things are put
away, all things become new."—II Corinthians 5:17. The
new birth paves the way for a person to take on the godly
traits of love, joy, long-suffering and patience and also enables him to put aside intolerance and bigotry. The new man
in Christ is better equipped than the most ardent social

reformer or religious do-gooder to bring about long-term and decisive, positive changes in the social structure.

This view has great potential pertinence for a place like Jackson, Mississippi, where manifestations of the new life in Christ have been sadly lacking in relationships between the races. And while Graham's first order of business, here as anywhere else in the world, will be to bring men to acceptance of Christ, the impact of his Jackson visit will also be evaluated in terms of how interpersonal and corporate racial attitudes have been modified or changed as a result of his ministry.

The Crusade office

Grady and Billy and I pile into the car and we head up North State Street to Woodrow Wilson Avenue where we make a left turn and pull up in front of the American Public Life Building. We walk up to the second floor, and fifty mouths open in surprise and shock when Billy enters the Crusade office. Everything stops except the incessant ring of the many telephones scattered around the office, while Billy goes up to each person and has a word of greeting and appreciation.

He seems genuinely interested in meeting these people. He has of course never seen them before, nor will he remember their names or likely ever see them again. Yet this is not a mechanical exercise suggested by a Madison Avenue brain. There really was no particular or pressing need to come to the headquarters, and indeed the time could have been better spent in rest or preparation for tomorrow's all-day meeting of the Billy Graham Evangelistic Association Executive Board where a number of urgent matters related to his 1976 schedule are to be discussed and adjudicated.

Nevertheless, Graham patiently signs autographs and then sits for a moment or two in Charlie Riggs's office and receives a briefing on platform arrangements for tonight's Johnny Cash visit.

One of the workers, a teen-age girl named Joyce Gomez, comes up to Graham and tells him about a friend who came to Christ the evening before. Joyce had been praying for this girl and she was thrilled with her friend's conversion and wanted to share the good news with Billy. Graham asked the girl's name and instructed Charlie Riggs to make sure that adequate follow-up was being employed.

Normally, an inquirer is contacted by a counselor by telephone, mail or personal visit within forty-eight hours of his coming forward at a Crusade service. It is of course quite impossible for Graham to keep track of his converts; it is up to the local committee and churches to effect follow-up and to insure that the individual is put in contact with a local congregation. He is, however, greatly interested in learning about individual conversions, and his mail reflects the variety of persons who come to Christ as a result of his ministry.

Graham has often been criticized for not staying in a community once a Crusade has ended to oversee follow-up personally, but not only is this logistically impossible, it runs counter to his own perception of his role as an evangelist. He sees himself as the catalyst, the agent used by God to bring a person who has been moved by the Holy Spirit to make a decision for Christ. This is his particular gift, and even his most severe critics must admit that he has been consistently faithful to this calling. Graham believes that the Christian ministry calls for a division of activities, and he feels it is up to others to provide the nurture that will transform the new convert into a mature believer.

Impact on the public at large

Still, unlike many evangelists who come into a town, win souls and then leave without establishing a mechanism for follow-up, the Graham organization provides the training and materials that will enable local Christians to conduct a successful follow-up campaign. Each inquirer receives *Decision* magazine and periodic letters from Graham for one year following the Crusade. When inquirers come forward they are given a booklet containing a correspondence course, *Knowing Christ*. Then they receive *Growing in Christ, Obeying Christ* and *Sharing Christ*, with additional

Bible study helps. Three weeks after the Crusade each inquirer is called to determine if he is attending a local church. The committee also sponsors a twice-daily radio Bible study program in an attempt to maintain the atmosphere of the Crusade until the local churches can assume the major burden of follow-up. It is just at this point that so many of his critics err when they advance "studies" and more often theories to prove that Graham converts do not last. The long-term nurture of a Graham-Crusade convert is not the responsibility of the Graham organization but lies within the province of the local churches. If converts do not grow in the Christian life, the blame lies with the churches and Christians in the new believer's neighborhood.

It is also true that despite claims to the contrary the great percentage of Graham converts do remain within the evangelical fold, and many become active, highly motivated believers. One has only to talk to a cross section of seminarians at evangelical schools or visit local congregations around the United States to gauge the tremendous impact Graham's ministry has had upon a very significant number of persons.

Many of Graham's critics are also shortsighted in the sense that they fail to note the impact Graham has upon the public at large. He is invariably the first person who comes to mind when one is asked to name the nation's most important religious leader, and his positions on many value-oriented issues such as pornography, the right to life, familial relationships and the whole range of social justice problems including race relations, poverty, hunger and public morality are of tremendous and, I would guess, increasing influence.

More than a preacher

Several years ago, a major politician said of Graham, "He is more than a preacher, more than an evangelist, more than a Christian leader. In a greater sense he has become our conscience."

This evaluation may go too far, but in a period when the pantheon of political and public leaders has been sorely depleted, Graham is one of the few remaining authoritative and respected national personalities. Unlike many instant celebrities he is not a creation of the media, and although he acknowledges the importance of the Hearst newspapers' coverage of the first Los Angeles Crusade in 1947, his great prestige has been built on a solid base of achievement over a thirty-year period.

Each of the major political parties has asked Graham on several occasions to run for office, and it is not far-fetched to assume that he could attract a large following if he decided to run for the nation's highest office. Two Presidents wanted Graham to serve in their Cabinets, and he could have his pick of any diplomatic or ceremonial post he might desire. Graham has resisted all of these offers and the temptation which certainly must have accompanied them, and in this he has displayed much good sense. Not only does he view himself as serving a higher power, but he also realizes that identification with a particular political party or acceptance of a specific governmental responsibility would diminish his spiritual effectiveness and ultimately weaken his organization and power base.

There are of course ordained clergy in the Congress, and two ministers worked in the White House. Billy Moyers, an ordained Southern Baptist, served under Johnson; and Father John McLaughlin, a Jesuit priest, labored in the vineyard of Richard Nixon. But none of these individuals have enjoyed the opportunities for direct Christian service that confront and challenge Graham.

It is now twelve-thirty and Charlie Riggs asks Graham if he would like to stop for a bite to eat before returning to the Holiday Inn. Billy says fine, let's go someplace nearby, and we all drive over to Morrison's Cafeteria, a popular low-priced restaurant located in an older subdivision near the Mississippi Memorial Stadium. It is almost impossible for Billy to complete a meal in a restaurant; people continually come over to his table wanting to talk or seeking an autograph, and the situation in Morrison's is fairly typical.

As Billy goes through the line—he is wearing a golf cap and dark glasses to avoid detection (recently someone gave him an airline pilot's hat, and he also has an old tweed number)—a murmur goes up from behind the serving counter, and no sooner is his soup placed on a tray then people begin to shout, "There's Billy Graham." We sit at a booth and people start to converge on Billy. Grady and Charlie, who have already put in a good day's work, are hungry and they quickly demolish their sandwiches, but

Billy is under siege and he only manages a couple of spoon-
fuls of chicken soup and a taste of salad.

One old lady is especially persistent—she wants Billy's
picture but unfortunately no one in the immediate vicinity
has a camera.

"Well, will you mail me one," she says, "and be sure it's
autographed."

Graham answers her with the unfailing good grace and
patience of one who has spent years in countless cafes listening to similar requests, and Grady jots the woman's name
and address down in a little binder notebook.

"I think it's time to go," Grady says, but Billy is already
up and shaking hands with people at the adjoining tables.
"Be sure to come out tonight; Johnny Cash will be singing
and I'm going to preach on the problems of young people,"
he tells a teen-age couple who have paused in their mutual
admiration of each other to look up at the evangelist.

"Charlie, give these folks a pass to the reserved section, I
know they're going to enjoy the service," Graham adds, and
in a few seconds he is out the door and standing by the car
waiting for the rest of us to catch up.

In the car I ask Graham if he is not bothered by this ce-
lebrity status, by the fact that he cannot go out to eat like an
ordinary person, that he cannot shop or engage in any everyday public activities without being stared at and stopped.
He is rather philosophical about the problem; he knows it
will never go away, and his only concern is that his witness
always remain courteous and Christ-like.

"I have been placed by God in a particular situation.
There are great pressures but also great rewards. The people
who come up to me and want to meet and talk to me normally do so from a legitimate motivation. I feel I should respond to them. Of course it is impossible to see everyone
and to listen to their concerns. Why, in Jackson alone I have
received two hundred and seventy-five requests for private
interviews and appointments. Obviously I cannot see but a
small fraction of these persons. I find I have to consider
prayerfully who I should see and how I should most effectively use my time. In my mind at all times is the desire to

glorify God in my actions and to be as fruitful as humanly possible in his service."

I ask Graham if in this age of assassination and physical attack people coming up to him in public places worry him. He replies that there is always the danger that a crazed person will attempt to do him harm—his closest call came years ago in San Diego, when a man came at him with a knife.

Security problems

Graham, like all well-known figures, must be something of a fatalist. There is little he can do to protect himself in a crowd and obviously he is an easy target for attack when preaching in huge open stadiums. His comments remind me of those attributed to President John Kennedy on the morning of his assassination, when he pointed to an early building and said, "A nut could easily shoot me from a rooftop."

As one who believes he has been called to reach as many men as possible for Christ, Graham cannot live in a shelter, he cannot hide his candle or even his body under a bushel, he must go out to the world's great cities and preach the gospel regardless of the personal dangers involved.

Our conversation reminds me of a talk I had with T. W. Wilson concerning an invitation Graham had received to hold a Crusade in a country that has had more than its share of political assassinations. I told T.W. that I feared for Billy's safety, but he also worried about himself. "After all, I'm the guy who will be standing next to Billy."

I have noticed that T.W. is normally an effective bodyguard in a crowd, and in Crusade settings Billy is usually protected by two or three plain-clothes detectives.

Vietnam echoes

Back at the hotel there are several urgent telephone messages awaiting Graham's attention. The most pressing call is from the island of Guam, where thousands of Vietnamese refugees have been taken on the first stop of their flight from their native land. Graham has been very much concerned with the plight of these unfortunate people. Although he has taken severe criticism in the past for not speaking out on the Indochina war, the evangelist has had a keen interest in Southeast Asia events, particularly the problem of human suffering precipitated by the bitter fighting.

Graham first became familiar with the Indochina situation during a 1962 visit with President Kennedy when the late President was vacationing at Palm Beach, Florida. Later he would be fully informed by his close friend President Johnson on the progress of the war, and Mr. Nixon also briefed the evangelist when they met in Washington or San Clemente.

From the mid sixties on, Graham was under great pressure from liberal Christians to speak out on the war, but he felt such comments would be indiscreet. He did go to Vietnam several times to minister to the troops, and on one occasion his visit coincided with a mission undertaken by the militantly pro-war Francis Cardinal Spellman of New York. Newsmen tried to get Graham to agree with the strongly favorable statements on U.S. policy issued by Spellman but Graham wisely demurred. Unfortunately the fact that the two religious leaders were present in Vietnam at the same time led some persons to believe their views were similar, and Graham was labeled a "hawk."

On the other hand, Graham certainly was worried about the possibility of a Communist takeover in Southeast Asia, and there is little question but that he supported American foreign policy during most of the 1960s. The many rallies, demonstrations and other anti-war incidents notwithstanding, he joined millions of Americans in holding this position.

Several of his critics tried to suggest that Graham was involved in policy making vis-à-vis the Vietnam conflict, but this was not at all true. He was informed by President Nixon of the invasion of Cambodia a few hours before that operation was launched, but he had no voice in the decision to broaden the scope of the war nor did he have any input on the bombing in Hanoi or other controversial aspects of the

American involvement. Graham was, and legitimately so, worried about the status of the many missionaries who had stayed on in Indochina long after the fighting began, and he did attempt to articulate the concerns of evangelicals over the fate of these Christian workers.

The refugee officials on Guam are urging Graham to suspend his current schedule and fly immediately to the island. They believe Graham can bring a message of comfort and hope to the many refugees who are stunned and disoriented by the rapid change in their fortunes. Graham is sorely tempted to say yes, but he cannot simply pick himself up and ask his associates to take over responsibility for the Jackson meetings. He recognizes the importance of his presence at the Crusade. There is nothing of a sense of pride or arrogance here—long experience has taught that the people are coming out to see and hear Billy Graham, the entire effort which has been five years in the making is built around him and while there are a number of competent preachers who could fill in for him, if he were to leave, the Crusade would lose its focus, its basic raison d'être.

Yet Graham cannot summarily reject the Guam request. He has Grady Wilson working on possible schedule changes; Grady checks flight tables, the question of time changes, how many days it would take to fly out, meet and speak to the refugees, fly home to keep important commitments. The Crusade will end Sunday afternoon; could he leave for Guam immediately after the closing service? Well, Jackson is not the easiest place in the world to fly out of on a Sunday and, more important, he is to be honored in Charlotte on Tuesday as the "Man of the South." On a personal level this accolade is relatively unimportant to Graham, but President Ford is coming for the event and the evangelist cannot cancel out. Billy talks to a high ranking U.S. representative on Guam and informs him of the severe logistical problems involved in changing his schedule, but he promises to continue checking to determine if he could come over during the next seven to ten days. Ultimately Graham will not be able to travel to Guam, but he and

Grady Wilson spend a considerable amount of time talking by telephone with refugee officials and Christian leaders on the island.

Integrated team

It is now one-fifteen and Graham has several individual appointments scheduled. He asks T. W. Wilson to take care of the other important phone calls and he directs his secretary to hold all other calls until further notice. There is a knock on the outer door and Dr. E. V. Hill, pastor of the Mount Zion Baptist Church in South Central Los Angeles and the first black member of the BGEA Board, walks in. Hill is a massive man and he greets Billy with a bear hug.

"Ed, how have you been, how are things in Watts?" Graham asks.

"I'm just great, Billy, and I need to talk to you about some people I think should be interviewed for your staff."

Several months before at a meeting of his organization's board of directors, Graham indicated that he wished to add more blacks to his staff, and Hill, who has wide contacts within the black evangelical community, has been busy identifying qualified candidates.

Hill and Graham first met during the 1963 Los Angeles Crusade. During the next several years Hill would read about Billy's activities, and although the two men were not in personal touch, Hill was very much interested in Graham's position on the race issue. Hill had heard several conflicting appraisals of Graham and he wanted to find out for himself where the evangelist stood on this vital national question. When Graham came to Anaheim, California, for a 1969 Crusade, Hill as an important local pastor was invited by the Crusade committee to offer a prayer during a service. He sat behind the evangelist, and when the Benediction had been given he tapped Graham on the shoulder and blurted out, "Billy, I've got to talk you." To his great surprise Graham responded, "I've got to talk to you." A week later Hill was summoned to Huntington Beach where Graham was resting following the Crusade.

Hill drove down to the resort determined "to actually know Billy Graham. I had heard much about him from others but I never look at a person through other people's eyeglasses, I use my own." Although the appointment was scheduled to last thirty minutes, the two men met for over four hours. Hill recalls, "We prayed together, we cried together, we became friends and I've been a close-up supporter ever since."

Now sitting on a green couch in Graham's hotel room, Hill tells the evangelist how delighted he was to see so many blacks at the previous night's service.

"I've been spending my time meeting with the brothers. A lot of my brothers have many questions about you, Billy; they want to know about your true intentions and whether the Graham organization is trying to engulf us as a race. I say to them you have to understand Billy Graham as being involved in a four-base ministry. The first-base ministry is reconciling man to God, but once you've reached first you don't turn right and go back into the dugout. You turn left and go on to second base where reconciled men under God become reconciled one to another. But you can't stay on second and make love all day, because at third base we hear the cries of the poor and hungry, and if we did not move on to third we would make a farce of our reconciliation. So we move to third and try to ameliorate human distress, but we don't stop there because Billy has a home-plate ministry and that's to anticipate the coming of the Lord, to know that we are heavenbound—that's home plate.

"You remember, Billy," he says, "I predicted this would probably be your most integrated Crusade. The reason I said this is that the true story of the South has not been told. The last time I was in Jackson, Mississippi, was with the Freedom Riders. It's a long way from this hotel to where I stayed in those days."

Billy laughs and then turns serious. "Ed, you have been a tremendous blessing to our work, and I know you have met with a number of pastors to explain my ministry and my reasons for coming to Jackson. I so much appreciate all you have done."

At this stage in their conversation they turn to a discussion of the names on Hill's list and I excuse myself and wander down to the lobby where I will wait for Hill. I want to put some questions to him concerning the level of integration here and the reaction of the black pastors to the Crusade. Twenty-five minutes later I see Hill emerge from the elevator and I ask if he has a few moments to chat with me. He nods yes and we go up to his third-floor room.

I instinctively know that one can be totally frank and open with Hill. There is in the man no semblance of guile or pretense, there is also a no-nonsense aura about him, so I come quickly to the point. The Crusade is integrated, even impressively so, but will the euphoria of eight days last down the long months and years ahead? I, too, remember what Jackson used to be. The city was widely recognized as the last major bastion of resistance to the currents of racial change alive in other parts of the nation.

People praying together

Mississippi played a major role in the history of the fifties and sixties. One recalls the Emmett Till case, the murder of the three civil rights workers at Philadelphia, the furor raised by the matriculation of James Meredith at the University of Mississippi, murder of Medgar Evers and, in more recent days, the tragedy of Jackson State. Given this background, is it possible that Billy Graham can make an impact on the course of race relations in the state?

Hill looks me in the eye and says, "The answer to your question is yes. I don't know of any other movement which does as much lasting good in a community as a Billy Graham Crusade. I don't know of anything else that touches as many people as a Graham Crusade. A year ago people who didn't know each other started praying together, started studying together, started planning together; it brought people together along racial lines. Now you see integration in the choir, on the platform, in stands. We've talked about it in the past, we said it ought to happen, it needs to happen but somehow the Billy Graham Evangelistic Association has made it happen."

Hill's words echo comments made by local black-and-white clergymen. Black minister Herman Pride, the Crusade treasurer, in commenting on the value of the prayer groups said, "This has been the first time that many black people have entered white churches. They have begun to know one another. The Crusade has brought them together."

Another Crusade official, Dr. S. L. Bowman, long active in civil rights, stated, "People have gotten to know each other across racial lines. This had not happened prior to the Crusade."

When asked to comment on the racial aspects of the Crusade, the Reverend Donald Patterson, pastor of the all-white First Presbyterian Church, said, "We have blacks and whites on our committee and we have been blessed of God with a good relationship. The Crusade has helped us move in the right direction."

But, I insist, what of the future? Will these pastors continue to meet together or will they go their own way as has been the case in the past?

Hill responds with real force. "When we leave here normal problems will crop up but we now have a precedent and when problems occur the people here can say, we worked together on the Billy Graham Crusade, we can work together on this. I think the Crusade has established an open door for black and white pastors to relate."

I now turn the subject of conversation to Graham himself. I am curious to learn what Hill thinks of Graham the man. His insights will be interesting, because unlike many on the Graham Association's board and Team, Hill does not go back to the old days when lifetime ties were cemented; he is in a position to be more objective than the others in his evaluation of the evangelist.

"I've been around a lot of people in and out of the church who have experienced considerable success and I've learned that there is something about success and power which tends to corrupt, but when you look at the Billy Graham Association, when you look at Billy, when you look at Ruth and their children, when you go into their homes, when you knock on the door, you expect to meet someone who supersedes the Apostle Paul, a holier than thou, and here comes a smiling down-home person from North Carolina who just grabs you and says, 'Hello, brother.' You're shocked but it's a glad shock. On the one hand you expected someone you would bow to; on the other hand you have someone you can say to, 'Hey, give me a piece of chicken.' And I think this is why God has chosen to continue to use him. I believe it is those who remain simple and down to earth and humble and touchable that he has chosen to manifest his glory through.

"And I'll tell you something else," Hill continues, "Billy has the lowest ratings of Billy Graham of any polls that have been taken. I don't know anybody who is more critical of Billy Graham than Billy Graham himself. When I first realized this I thought he was jiving me but this was not so; this man does not do things with the certainty that 'I'm Billy Graham and people are going to listen to me.' I don't think he's ever had the thought 'Well, I'm Billy Graham and I'm going to Rio and two hundred thousand people are going to meet me there and I'm going to slay them.' His attitude is, 'Well, we will do good if twenty thousand show up.'"

I ask Hill what there is about Graham that has enabled him to be a pace setter, to move his constituents forward on key theological and social issues. Hill leans forward in his chair and smiles. "Look, I think Billy is often surprised himself at what he says and does. There are often aftershocks that follow his actions, but the true man of God, when questioned as to whether he really meant to say or do a certain thing, says 'Yes, I did mean it,' while the fake says 'Well, wait a minute—that action needs interpretation.' Billy as a true servant of God listens for his voice and has the courage to say and do what God has told him."

I have a final question for E. V. Hill: How long can or will Billy maintain his ministry? Will he continue to preach and hold Crusades into the indefinite future?

Hill replies, "Time and circumstances are going to keep Billy involved in Crusades whether he wants to or not. The nation has lost confidence in many institutions, but Billy has retained his credibility, and people, especially young people, will continue to talk to Billy and Billy's going to constantly respond to them. I don't think he wants this responsibility. I can't really blame him, because it's an awesome responsibility, but being the kind of man he is and knowing the way he walks with God, he will continue to speak out and he will keep busy for a long time to come."

I am greatly impressed by Hill and by the force of his personality; I can understand why Graham has allied himself with Hill—I see this relationship as one more example of the evangelist's propensity to add able, highly competent people to his organization. He certainly has chosen his black colleagues well.

Howard Jones, an associate evangelist since 1958, and Ralph Bell, a talented graduate of Taylor University, have made important contributions to the Graham ministry, while Norman Sanders, Jones's son-in-law, has impressed the Jackson community with his expertise as a Crusade associate. These aides and other blacks close to the Graham organization intuitively trust Graham on the race issue and they are aware of his behind-the-scenes effort on behalf of the black struggle for equality.

In the late 1960s Graham invited a score of black church leaders to meet with him in New York for a frank off-the-record discussion of their problems. During the session, several of the black participants expressed concern over the Nixon administration's plan to cut off funds for social welfare projects. They also were troubled by their inability to communicate directly with the Chief Executive. Graham arranged for a number of the pastors to meet with Nixon in the White House. As a result of this session, Nixon aides reinstated significant funds for black neighborhood programs.

One participant in the Oval Office meeting, Rev. John Williams of Kansas City (now a member of the BGEA board), mentioned to the President that funds needed to complete a hospital in his area were frozen. Two days later Williams received word that the Department of Health, Education and Welfare had approved a one-million-dollar grant for the project. Today the Martin Luther King Hospital provides vital services to the Kansas City black community.

On the other hand, Graham's black associates also know that Graham's stand on race has cost him friends and finances.

When Howard Jones first came on the staff, Graham received a number of letters asking why he was associating with "niggers." Graham, however, would make a special point of introducing Jones at meetings and receptions. It must be remembered that the American churches until well into the sixties were highly segregated institutions. Indeed it used to be said that 11 A.M. Sunday morning was the most segregated hour of the week. The evangelical churches were especially prone to discrimination; this in part was due to a generally accepted notion that the Bible taught Negroes were inherently inferior to whites.

Billy Graham, who grew up in a region highly permeated by such teachings, had to wait until he went up to Wheaton College to be disabused of this doctrine. At the Illinois school his anthropology teacher, Dr. George Horner, enabled Graham to understand that there was no scientific basis for the theory of Negro inferiority and it was a lesson he would never forget. When Graham came to Jackson in 1953 to conduct a four-week Crusade he insisted on integrated seating. He also made a number of public comments on race that worried the city and state's power structure and caused the then governor, Hugh White, to telephone and urge Billy to stop speaking out on the racial issue. Howard Jones recalls the late Dr. Martin Luther King, Jr., telling Billy, "I believe your Crusades are doing more to break down racial barriers and to bring the races together than what I'm doing. Your work is helping me."

CHAPTER 4   THE INCREDIBLE
             SCHEDULE

It is now two thirty-five, and when I go back upstairs to
Graham's suite I find him meeting with Sterling Huston, the
Team member who is responsible for all of Graham's Crusades and speaking engagements in North America. Walter
Smyth, who has been with the Graham organization since
1950, formerly held this position, but he now directs the international aspects of the Graham ministry.

Huston is a tall, good-looking, thirty-five-year-old native of
Maine who like many of his older colleagues in the Graham
organization came to the BGEA from the professional ranks
of Youth for Christ. He is an engineer by training with a
master of science degree in paper and pulp technology and
several years of business experience with major corpora-
tions. It is to Huston's attention that the majority of requests
for Graham's public time come, and he then is responsible
for the exploration, preparation, function and follow-up of
Crusades and other speaking dates. It is Huston's unhappy

task to say no to the overwhelming majority of the more than eight thousand requests Graham receives each year.

Huston has had to answer negatively to an increasing extent in the last year. This is because Graham has felt the need to limit his schedule more than in the past. He simply cannot go for sixteen weeks at a stretch as in the first New York City Crusade, and he is not able to preach two and three times a day as he once did.

Graham usually conducts five major Crusades a year. Two or three are held within the United States, with other Crusades taking place in major world centers such as West Germany, Hong Kong or Australia. In addition, Graham will speak at college and university commencements, important gatherings like the annual meeting of the Southern Baptist Convention and in key pulpits such as New York's Riverside Church.

Graham also presides over the quarterly board meetings of the Billy Graham Evangelistic Association, and he spends many days each year at board sessions of institutions such as Gordon College and Divinity School and in visiting projects administered by members of his Team.

Part of each week is given over to his "Hour of Decision" radio broadcast, and several hours in any given week are devoted to writing his daily newspaper column as well as to magazine articles and an occasional book.

In addition to all of this, there are visits to family and old friends, meetings with top political, social and economic leaders and hours of study and meditation both for personal spiritual needs and as preparation for the scores of sermons and messages Graham must deliver during the course of the year.

Sterling Huston writes regular brief memos to Billy giving him the latest information on scheduling and the progress of planning for upcoming engagements, and it is in reaction to one of these memoranda that Billy has called Huston to his suite. He wants some more information concerning his upcoming appearance before the national convention of the American Bar Association. Billy had been asked on two other occasions to take this assignment, but each time he was occupied and unable to accept.

Later in the year he will speak to over one thousand atomic scientists at Los Alamos, the first time this influential body has been addressed by a clergyman.

Huston tells Billy that the August ABA date is firm and that Billy should arrive in Montreal, the site of the meeting, in time for a 1 P.M. reception. He then advises Billy of the progress of the Washington, D.C., Crusade scheduled for mid-1976.

Hope for a spiritual renewal of America

Graham is especially interested in the national Bicentennial observance. He plans to spend all of 1976 in the United States and he has been swamped with requests for participation in Bicentennial-oriented events. Billy adds that he hopes the Bicentennial will result in a return to those religious principles he believes were basic to the founding and development of the nation.

This is a sensitive area for Graham; he has often been accused of promoting what the sociologist Robert Bellah calls, "American Civil Religion." Graham's participation in the White House religious services during the Nixon years and his leadership in the evangelical campaign known as "Key '73" have led some critics to charge that Graham promotes a religion of Americanism.

Graham has refuted these assertions, saying that his ministry is of world-wide dimensions and that anyway he does not represent the United States or any individual nation; instead he refers to himself as an "Ambassador for Christ."

There may be a fine line here between Graham's patriotism and love for America and the somewhat jingoistic events with which he is sometimes associated. Thus in 1970 he joined comedian Bob Hope and *Reader's Digest* President Hobart Lewis in sponsoring "Honor America Day." This Washington-based celebration, complete with a morning religious service and an evening fireworks display, was apparently aimed at articulating what the sponsors believed was right with America at a time when many young people and some of their elders were discovering many things wrong with their country.

Graham, in a legitimate rendering of his basic message, in his speech to the thousands of persons assembled before the Lincoln Memorial, called his audience and the nation to spiritual renewal. Others, however, including the then President, Nixon, used Honor America Day to "prove" that all was well with American society. Now, in a conversation with me, the evangelist indicates that his Bicentennial activity will not be open to the critique that he equates Christianity with America or American values.

How team members are selected

Huston and Billy also discuss some personnel questions. Obviously a position with the Graham organization calls for a special kind of person, one who combines professional expertise with deep spiritual commitment. When I later ask Sterling Huston what he looks for in a prospective Team member, he responds that the Graham ministry has a sense of mission to it. Therefore the person "must be motivated by his commitment to Christ." The candidate must also have an attitude that is "consistent with the spirit and drive that Mr. Graham exemplifies."

I ask if this does not make for persons who will attempt to imitate Graham, but Huston quickly replies that this is the last thing Billy wants.

"We're not looking for little Billy Grahams but rather men who have a sense of woe if they do not preach the gospel."

I find this an interesting response, for while I have over the years run across many preachers and church workers who, whether consciously or not, affect almost all of Graham's mannerisms and vocal inflections, I cannot think of a single Team member who reminds me of Billy in either his public or his private life.

Then Huston adds that, in addition to spiritual qualities and vocational ability, the Graham organization looks for people who make a good appearance—"not that appearance makes one a better man, but it reduces the limitations a man faces if he is to present himself well."

Anyone looking at the Team and the immediate support staff will quickly notice their tasteful dress, neat appearance and cheerful demeanor. I ask why the people around Billy Graham are so serene and seem to get such satisfaction from their work, and Huston replies that the Team members believe that being with Billy is exactly where God wants them. They feel they are involved in an exciting and productive ministry and that God really has called Billy to accomplish great things. They also find in Billy the qualities of sincerity, dedication and honesty.

I have been told stories by Team members of individual acts of generosity by Graham and of the special concern he has for their wives and children. During my conversations with him I am struck by the many times he favorably mentions staff and his praise for their activities. I have also been impressed by the Team members' loyalty to Billy. While his associates are not hesitant to admit his points of weakness and to criticize his performance constructively when they feel this is appropriate, they are also his greatest boosters, and their continuing relationship with him despite attractive and even lucrative offers to go elsewhere is perhaps the greatest single testimony to his ability to lead and set a proper tone for the work of the association.

Huston seems to sum this up when he says, "When you're related to someone whom God has particularly chosen and he has been generous and gracious, there's not a lot of room for conflict."

When Huston leaves I ask Graham if he is not frustrated by having to refuse so many invitations and speaking opportunities. He says that he does feel enormous pressures and he is unhappy over his inability to visit many of the world areas that urgently request his presence, but he also realizes that Jesus' active ministry lasted for only three years and yet when he went to the cross he was able to say, "It is finished."

I get the impression that despite the frustrations, Graham believes he is "running the race" described by Paul in the

New Testament to the best of his intellectual ability and physical capacity. There is also the certainty in his mind that whatever he does has been directed by God as a result of prayer and the leading of the Holy Spirit. Therefore he will not say, "We should have gone to Dallas last month instead of to Munich." Billy may linger over a decision; he will want the best input and advice available, but once the commitment has been made he will hold to it and give the assignment his very best.

The very fact of his fame and the assumption that he receives so many more invitations than he can possibly take inhibit some persons who might stand a good chance of an acceptance from even petitioning for his services. Sometimes, as I learn from talking to Graham, this leads to misunderstandings. He asks me why a certain religious leader with whom we are mutually acquainted has invited a member of the Team rather than Billy himself to address a theological colloquium. Billy wants to know if this official is angry with him, and he is hard-pressed to know what the cause of anger might be. I assure Graham that the person is not upset with him but rather felt that it would be better not to put Billy on the spot by inviting him to attend a function that probably would not have a high priority on his schedule. Billy understood, but I wonder if he really comprehends the reserve that people who know him develop because of their knowledge of his complex ministry and the great demands on his time.

Sometimes it takes a good measure of old-fashioned *chutzpa* to ask Billy for an appointment, and yet there are occasions when a person instinctively knows that Billy will respond positively to a request regardless of the pressures involved. I had this experience several years ago when Rivka Alexandrovich, a Soviet Jewish woman from the city of Riga, came to the United States to attempt to win public support for her daughter, Ruth, then a prisoner of conscience in Russia. I called Billy one afternoon and reached him in the barbershop of Washington's Madison Hotel. After hearing of Mrs. Alexandrovich's problem, Billy invited me to bring her to Chicago in two days' time so he could

meet and talk with her. The Chicago session was packed
with emotion. There was a definite positive chemistry alive
in the room, and Billy expressed great sympathy for young
Ruth Alexandrovich. At one point in the conversation he
walked to the telephone, took out an address book and
dialed a long-distance number.

"Is Henry there?" he asked. "Well, tell him to call me the
minute he comes in."

No one in the room had to ask who "Henry" was, and
there was little doubt in our minds that the call had been
placed to Key Biscayne, Florida, where Henry was staying
with his boss, the President of the United States.

Five minutes later the telephone rang and it was Henry.
Graham gave him a briefing on Mrs. Alexandrovich (he had
carefully jotted down the pertinent facts as she talked) and
he then asked the caller to try to do something for the distraught émigré. Later that night Graham issued a statement
from his Minneapolis headquarters calling attention to the
plight of the Soviet Jews. Two months after the Chicago
meeting, Ruth Alexandrovich landed at Lod Airport in Tel
Aviv.

High demands of a telecast

I look at my watch; it is three-eleven and I tell Billy I will
see him again just before it is time to leave for the stadium.
This is no magnanimous gesture on my part; I have been
told in advance that Billy needs two hours in the afternoon
to prepare for his evening message and this period is virtu-
ally inviolate. Graham uses this time to rest, look over his
sermon and make any changes he feels necessary. This re-
view is particularly crucial when, as will be the case tonight,
his message is being taped for television.

When Billy prepares for television he in essence memo-
rizes his message so that he can look directly into the camera rather than at his notes. He must also be extremely careful in what he says, because the message will eventually be
viewed in many parts of the world. Local allusions must be
dropped; people watching the broadcast in India or Latin

America cannot be expected to know where Jackson is located, let alone understand what Graham means when he talks about "Ole Miss."

Graham must also articulate a message that can be theologically clear to people of varying spiritual backgrounds, and he must be aware that his audience will have different national, ethnic and racial components.

The addition of television to his Crusade ministry has placed great strains upon the evangelist, and the three or four days of each Crusade that are televised are usually quite tense for Graham and his associates. The television ministry represents an enormous investment of time, effort and money, and Graham is a very zealous steward of all of these commodities. Even his closest associates cannot fully comprehend what it costs Graham in physical, mental and emotional terms to preach before the camera. Once during a Crusade in Norfolk, Virginia, Graham took sick and was unable to go to the auditorium for one of the services. Grady Wilson, who took over the assignment, vividly recalls how taxing he found the experience of speaking to a live and world-television audience at the same time.

The quality of undiluted enthusiasm

When I return to the hotel lobby I find Harold Lindsell preparing to go over to the Team headquarters at the Jackson Hilton, and we share a taxi. Lindsell has had a fifteen-minute meeting with Graham, and while their conversation was privileged, Lindsell does tell me that the evangelist is very troubled over the world situation. (Two hours later the news will give dramatic substance to Graham's concern.) He has recently received information pointing toward a renewal of hostilities in the Middle East and he worries over the future of American involvement in the Pacific and on the Asian continent.

I am interested in this account of their conversation but I can't help thinking about Graham, up there in his hotel room getting ready for the evening meeting. I mention this to Lindsell and ask him a question that has been on my mind ever since I left Graham. After all the places he's been, all the experiences he's had, all the great and near-great people he's met, isn't it something of a letdown to come to a city like Jackson, doesn't he have to "psych" himself up to conduct a Crusade here?

Lindsell answers that this could be expected—Jackson is surely not one of the garden spots of the world, and even the challenges and opportunities here are different from what Graham would encounter in, say, Japan or South Africa or Germany, except that Graham has the quality of "undiluted enthusiasm," and this makes every Crusade or appearance fraught with meaning and purpose. "He is a man who genuinely relishes getting up in the morning, who lives with a constant air of expectancy."

It is also true that from a practical point of view it is important for Graham to appear from time to time in the Bible Belt. Jackson is very fertile territory, there is a tremendous density of evangelical Christians within a one- or two-hundred-mile radius and it is vital for Graham from time to time to touch base with the core element of his constituency.

The Hilton lobby is noisy and crowded and I soon discover that the commotion is due to the arrival of Johnny Cash, June Carter and their entourage. The Cashes and the Grahams are close, and Johnny usually tries to perform at Graham Crusades when his crowded schedule permits.

Cash's appearance at the Jackson Crusade is no simple matter of his flying into town with a few back-up musicians. Cash takes the Crusade date very seriously. He will have twenty people with him on the platform and he has brought all of the sound and lighting equipment he would normally use at a major paid performance. In fact, a huge truck containing these materials is now being unloaded at the stadium, and a crew of technicians is setting up the complicated paraphernalia that Cash employs in his act. Johnny and June are quickly hustled into an elevator and some of the lobby noise dies down.

Don Bailey, Graham's press representative, who has been unsweringly kind to me during my stay, brings over an attractive young woman and introduces her as an aide to Senator Goldwater. The girl's name in Claire Beversluis and she is the Arizonian's legislative secretary. She and her family rededicated their lives to Christ at the 1969 Madison Square Garden Crusade and she has since become an ardent Graham supporter. This is her sixth Crusade; she spends her vacations attending the meetings and helping out with office and counseling chores.

I later find there are a number of people who regularly come to the Crusades. These are not hero-worshipers or camp followers, but people who enjoy the fellowship and spiritual nourishment a Crusade provides. One old-timer, Peck Gunn, the self-styled poet laureate of Tennessee, brings a busload of friends to every U.S. Crusade, and his Tennessee ham breakfast is a must for the Team. If the Graham Team is like a family, Claire Beversluis, Gunn and the other regular Crusade attendees make up the extended Graham family. They manifest a healthy spirit of camaraderie and provide a welcome reservoir of familiar faces in the various locations to which the Team yearly travels.

It is four-thirty and Team members are returning from afternoon engagements. Howard Jones is back from the Parchman State Penitentiary where he preached to eight hundred convicts and saw two hundred confess Christ. Lee Fisher carries the accordion he used to entertain patients at a local nursing home, Walter Smyth has spent the afternoon meeting with Baptist officials, briefing them on the international aspects of the Graham ministry, while Cliff Barrows and Grady have been conducting a series of sessions with individuals who could not be fitted into the Graham schedule. In the press room, on the second floor, Arthur Matthews is talking to a UPI reporter in Washington and Don Bailey is sifting through interview requests from several national magazines.

Final preparations for the service

Two doors away T. W. Wilson and Charlie Riggs go over the program for this evening. T.W. is concerned about the weather; the sun has receded and ominous-looking dark clouds are building in the western sky. The Jackson area has been inundated with rain for the last three weeks. There has been considerable flooding in the outlying sections and the cotton crop may be delayed. For a time it appeared that the heavy rain would make the stadium infield too muddy for use by inquirers, but two days before the Crusade began the weather finally cleared and a warm sun dried out most of the turf. Now, however, it looks as if the precipitation is about to return. Adverse weather will have a definite impact upon the service. If the rain begins in the next hour or so many persons who had planned on coming to the service will likely remain at home. In this sense, although rain will discomfort the crowd in the open stadium, it is better if the wet weather arrives once the service has started.

On the other hand, there will be a base of about twenty thousand people present regardless of the elements. These are folk who have made advance reservations and are coming by bus. Although you cannot see or feel it, there is a sense of excitement and drama building in the Jackson area. People are returning home from offices, schools and factories, and in thousands of homes men, women and children are deciding whether or not to attend the Crusade session. In other thousands of homes, ushers, counselors, choir members, co-labor corps, operatives and a host of other Crusade volunteers are eating early suppers and making last-minute preparations to drive out to the stadium.

In the Jackson Hilton coffee shop, several Team members are enjoying a light snack, while over at the Holiday Inn North, the man who started the day with prayer ten hours ago is back on his knees asking God to give him a full measure of liberty and power for his message tonight.

When he has completed his prayers he turns on the TV to catch the five o'clock news and he learns that a group of pirates has seized the *Mayaguez*, an American merchant vessel operating in Cambodian waters. He then picks up the phone and makes a call to the Hilton. I am in my room when the telephone rings; it is Billy reminding me to meet Grady at five-fifty in front of the Holiday Inn.

Almost as an afterthought he adds, "Things are a lot more hectic today, Jerry, than when you were at the house." I am so stunned by the thoughtfulness involved in the call that I mumble something about, "Yes, it has been busy," and the conversation ends. I walk over to the window, and as I watch the clouds gather on the near horizon I think back several weeks to my trip to the evangelist's home.

CHAPTER 5   A FULL DAY AT
             HOME

Montreat is so tiny it does not appear on most road maps of
North Carolina. True, it is the home of the Presbyterian
Conference Grounds and Anderson-Montreat College, but
the first-time visitor to either of these facilities usually has to
ask for careful directions to find the retreat house or the
campus. Each year thousands of people take a left turn off
the main street of Black Mountain, a small village one and a
half miles west of Montreat, drive down a narrow tree-lined
road through the stone archway that says "Montreat," pass a
wooden and stone building that appears to be a large house
and then arrive at the Conference Center to study, swim,
relax and enjoy the beauty of the Blue Ridge. Most of these
persons do not realize that during the short ride from Black
Mountain to the Conference Grounds they have driven by
the office of Billy Graham, and they would be even more
surprised to learn that on the same ride they passed about a
thousand feet under the mountaintop home of the world-
renowned evangelist.

There are, of course, many people who do know that Billy Graham lives in Montreat, and some of these folk come to the hamlet from distant locations in the hope of meeting personally with Graham, but for the most part Graham is more associated with Minneapolis (just write to me, Billy Graham, Minneapolis, Minnesota he says at the conclusion of each "Hour of Decision" radio broadcast) than with the mountains of western North Carolina. Indeed, the only person of note normally associated with the region is the American novelist Thomas Wolfe, who was born in Asheville, a medium-sized city twenty miles to the west of Montreat, and whose boyhood home and grave site are tourist attractions for visitors to the Carolina mountain country.

Why live at Montreat?

Logic and coincidence come together to explain why Billy Graham lives in such a remote part of the United States. For a man who spends nine or ten months a year traveling to major population centers throughout the world, Montreat is a place of quiet, a serene oasis and shelter where Graham can rest and prepare for his incredibly complex and demanding public schedule. Montreat is also the place where Dr. and Mrs. L. Nelson Bell, Ruth Graham's parents, made their home upon their return from missionary service in China, and it was natural when Billy entered full-time evangelism and began to spend most of his time traveling that Ruth would want to settle close to her family.

The Grahams' first home was a small cottage located near the bottom of the mountain, and it was here that three of the five Graham children were born. Later Billy decided to build on the top of the slope, and although the evangelist has been entertained in presidential residences, imperial palaces, sumptuous mansions and the world's most famous and posh hotels, he is happiest when in his simple but spacious log house surrounded by family, his closest associates and the spectacular grandeur of the Blue Ridge Mountains.

At Montreat, Billy is also only a half hour by plane away from Atlanta, the headquarters of the Billy Graham Team;

Charlotte, his birthplace and the home of Grady Wilson, one of his two closest personal friends and associates; and Greenville, South Carolina, where Cliff Barrows, a key member of the Graham organization, makes his home.

It is a Monday morning in the early spring. Already the azaleas are beginning to blossom and the air is filled with a fragrant freshness. I left New York the evening before, flew into Charlotte, one of the South's most important commercial and industrial centers, rented a car and drove about fifty miles to Shelby, a crossroads at the edge of the mountains where I had dinner and spent the night. From Shelby the drive to Black Mountain took about an hour.

When I reached Black Mountain I found I was a half hour early for my appointment with Graham, so I walked through the two-block town center and bought the local newspaper. As far as I could determine no one in the village seemed preoccupied with the fact that less than two miles away lived a world-famous personality and the Gallup Poll's second most admired American. Not that I had expected to find kids hawking maps pointing to the Graham house, the way they do along Sunset Strip in Hollywood, directing tourists to the homes of the movie colony celebrities; or curio shops offering Graham photos or T-shirts; but at the least there could have been a signpost mentioning that this was Billy Graham's home. I talked to several townspeople and their answers to my questions concerning the proximity of Graham to them made it clear that having the evangelist in the neighborhood had no direct impact upon their lives.

Billy and Ruth are treated with respect and perhaps admiration by the local residents but so are the banker, editor and other successful people of the region. Folk in Black Mountain are more concerned with the price of agricultural commodities and the influx of mountain-loving tourists than with whether Billy is at home or on one of his frequent and lengthy trips.

At precisely ten o'clock I drive under the Montreat arch and turn left and then left again into the driveway of the modern colonial building that houses Graham's executive office. There I am greeted by Stephanie Wills, the evangelist's personal secretary, who directs me to the other side of the building where I am to meet T. W. Wilson, Billy's closest aide, and with his brother Grady one of Billy's oldest and most cherished friends.

T.W. is a large man whose serious face is highlighted by eyes that seem to say, "Who are you and why are you making demands on Billy's already impossible schedule?" It is T.W.'s job to serve as a buffer between the enormous number of people who want to reach Graham and the evangelist who must severely limit the amount of time he can give to any one person or group. (T.W. is also Billy's traveling companion and, aside from Grady, the one person he can most relax with when he is on the road.)

Best way to make an appointment

Anyone familiar with the Graham organization and its mode of operation knows that the best way to get in touch with Billy is through T.W., and this includes members of the Graham Team with only a few exceptions, such as Cliff Barrows and George Wilson, the executive vice-president and business manager of the Billy Graham Evangelistic Association.

T.W. lives in Billy's shadow—relatively few people outside of the Graham organization know of him, although he is a forceful and convincing preacher in his own right. T.W. accepts his role with genuine equanimity and understands that he must remain outside the public glare that surrounds Graham. He serves Billy faithfully and competently and at significant sacrifice to his personal and family life.

Like several of Graham's key associates, T.W. long ago could have formed his own organization and gained recognition in the evangelical community, but he has remained loyal to Billy and secure in the belief that God wants him at Billy's side. T.W. is impressive, not just physically but also intellectually and emotionally. He is the kind of man you instinctively trust and respect, and in that sense he is typical of the men Graham has chosen to surround himself with. There is in T.W.'s make-up an inner stability and a strong fiber of integrity that characterizes so many of Graham's people.

T.W. understands the world, he is daily exposed to the foibles of his fellows, he knows from personal experience the lengths to which people will go to attempt to exploit his boss or use him for ill or even self-assumed good causes, but there is a kind of unshakable confidence that what he does for Billy is important and meaningful. There is also more often than not a twinkle in T.W.'s eyes and a good measure of honest southern charm that makes one feel at home. This morning T.W. comes out of his large, functional office to meet me. He shows me around the facility, the library where Billy keeps his research materials, the projection room where Billy views the rushes from the latest World Wide Pictures (a Graham subsidiary) film projects, the storage room where the mementos and gifts of three decades of world recognition are carefully catalogued and kept, the large but comfortable upstairs meeting room where Billy entertains groups too large to be brought up to his house.

As I listen to Wilson it begins to dawn on me that the life of Billy Graham is far more complex and difficult than most people could possibly imagine. I also cannot help but wonder what makes Billy Graham tick, what is there in his character and psyche that makes him want to engage in his strenuous ministry and what resources are available to enable him to sustain his exhausting and demanding life-style. Surely I won't be able to discover all of the answers to these questions, but perhaps I will be able to come to some kind of conclusions about Graham's motivations and inner compulsions.

I am startled back to reality by the sound of Wilson's voice. He is talking to someone in the Graham house, and apparently Billy, who had been dictating to Stephanie Wills, is now ready to receive me. We leave T.W.'s office and climb into a late-model station wagon. T.W. drives out of

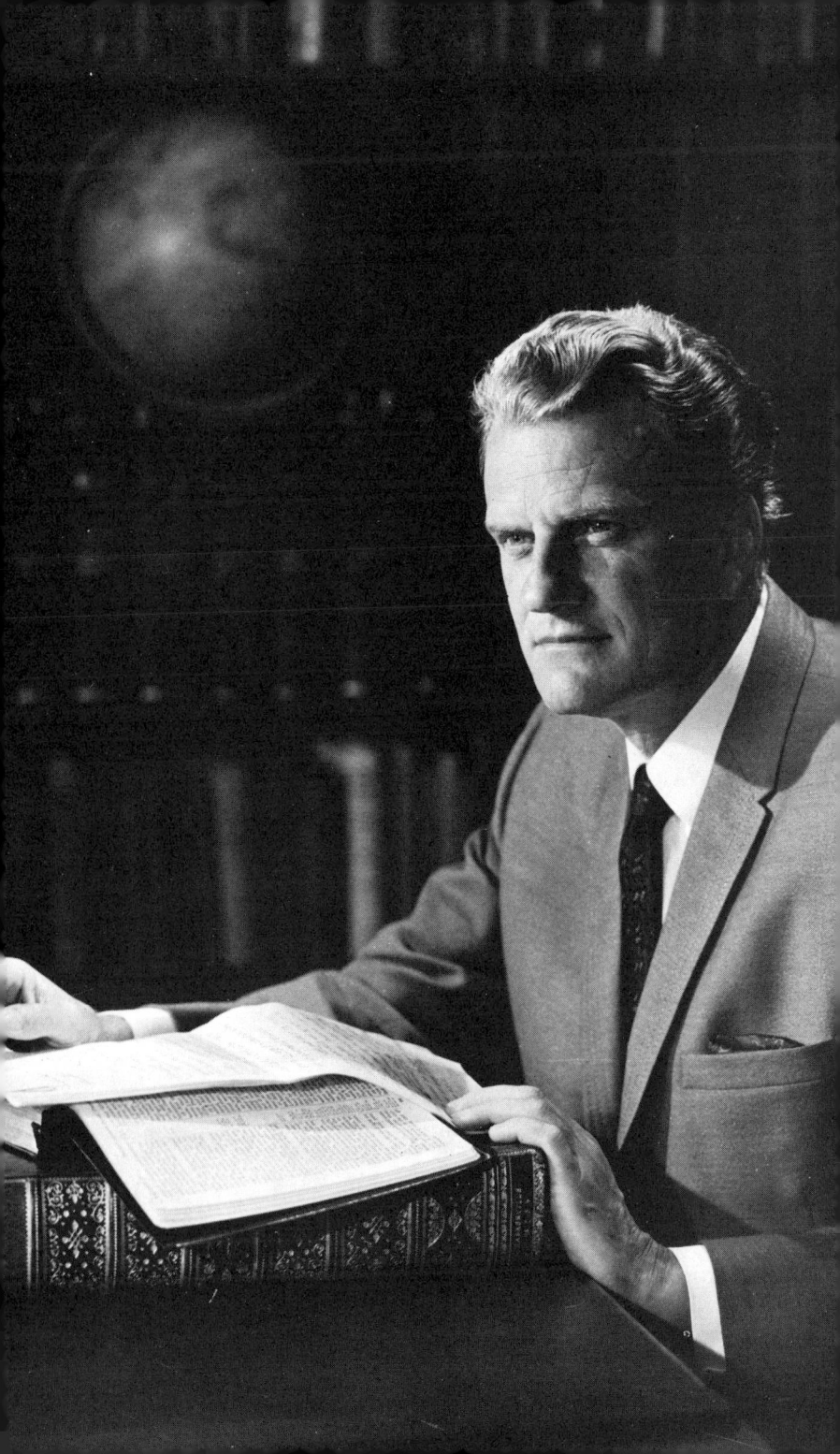

On the porch at home, relaxing with a glass of lemonade

Working on correspondence with an aide

AT
HOME
IN
MONTREAT

Posing with Ruth Graham

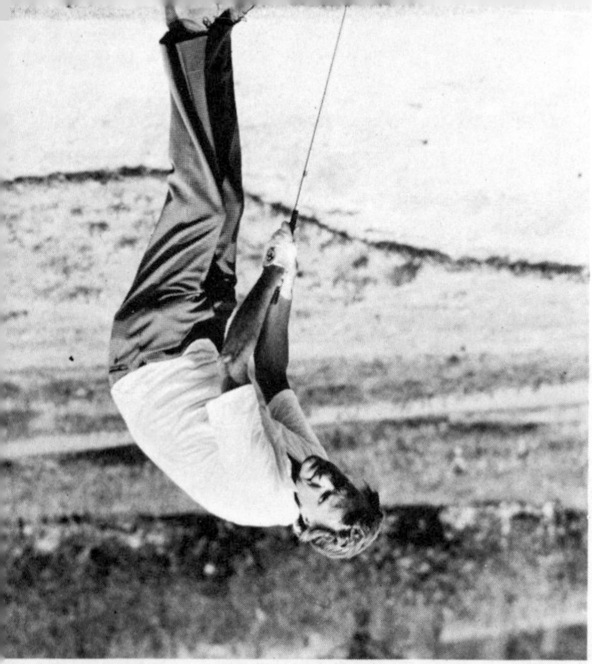

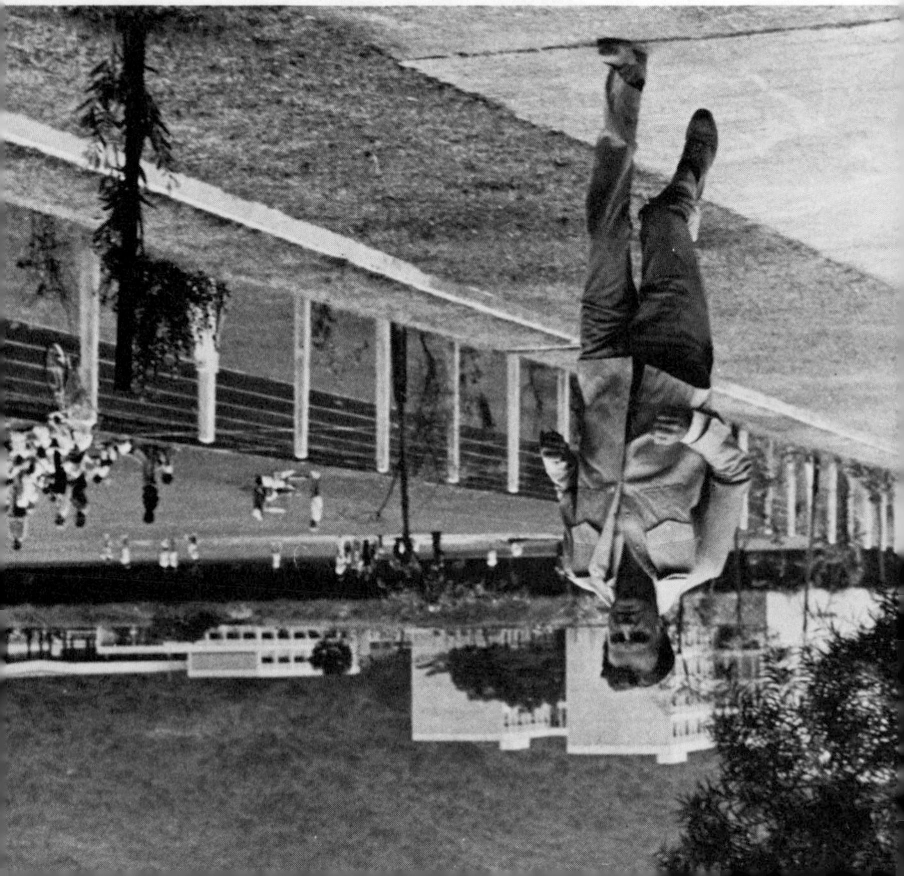

the parking area and turns onto a narrow road that circles
the mountain. The view is lovely even if we seem to be
perched on the side of a steep cliff. After five minutes we
come to a large gate that blocks the road. T.W., who has
been in constant radio communication with the Graham
house, touches a switch attached to the automobile's sun
visor and the gate is electronically opened. He explains this
is a security measure, and I can well understand the need
for the Grahams to be protected from unwanted visitors in
the isolated area of the mountain we are now entering.

The road continues to curve and push upward, and then
we come to a clearing and the path abruptly ends in a small
driveway. To the left, I see two cars, one a two- or three-
year-old Oldsmobile, the other a nearly new Datsun. I later
discover that the Olds belongs to Billy, while Ruth drives
the foreign model. As we leave the station wagon I hear
loud barking and I turn and see two large German shep-
herds running and jumping behind a fence. T.W. then takes
my arm and leads me to the entrance of the house. I look up
and am most pleasantly surprised to see Billy Graham waiting in the doorway.

Disarming personality

I am impressed by Graham's intense physical attractiveness. Although he is in his late fifties, Graham looks
healthy, alert and quite handsome. He is tall and slim, with
a mane of blond-gray hair, a long deeply tanned face, per-
fect white teeth and blue eyes. He has aged very well, his
maturity and the lines in his face have erased the boyish
look of photographs taken earlier in his career. When you
look at him closely his visage easily passes the test of time
and you recognize that portion of his success which must be
credited to the good looks with which he has been blessed.

When he smiles, as he often does, his face takes on a
bright glow and the cold and remote look that television at
times gives him is replaced by an unusual alertness and an
acute sense of physical well-being. It is as if his face and

body were meant to be attractive, complimenting his charismatic gift, his quick and agile mind and his tremendous communicative powers. One almost thinks it is too good to be true—no one his age has a right to look this way except perhaps Gregory Peck or Burt Lancaster.

Graham's physical attractiveness and the personality beneath have the capacity to disarm the stranger, to put from one's mind the difficult questions one should ask, to dispel the notions of doubt concerning the man's ultimate values and beliefs. Yet there is to Graham an innocence and an aura of honesty that quickly cause the visitor to see that this is a genuine person, not a fabricated, well-packaged product programed to please, disarm or charm.

Graham, who is dressed in tan slacks, a sports shirt and a dark brown sweater, leads me into the house. We pass through a hallway filled with paintings and photographs and memorabilia, and enter a very large, comfortable-looking room that is dominated by a huge stone fireplace. Graham and I sit on opposite couches. T. W. Wilson, who has followed us into the house, says he must return to the office and that he will check with us later. I feel the need to remind Billy why I am here, but he quickly assures me that he understands my purpose in coming and he adds that he will do everything he can to make my visit worth while. I tell him that he should feel free to ask me to leave his company if he is discussing confidential matters either by telephone or with visitors or staff, but he laughs and says that there is very little if anything he would not want me to hear. I am struck by the innate generosity of the man, not only for giving me the time to observe him but also because he has the gift of making one feel at ease.

As he talks I become relaxed and begin to believe that perhaps my presence will not be too much of an intrusion. I also realize that Billy Graham is very much in command of himself and that he fully understands his many responsibilities and that no one, however fine his motivation or however noble his purpose, is going to be able to inhibit Graham from what he feels he must do or accomplish.

Busy day

We begin our discussion by going over the day in outline. This is an especially busy time for the evangelist; he has a great deal of correspondence to catch up with, he must continue work on the second draft of his book on angels (the manuscript is already due at the publisher's), he has a backlog of at least thirty phone calls to answer, he needs to go over a week of newspaper columns, he must tape two messages for the "Hour of Decision," his press representative, Don Bailey, is coming up from Atlanta later today to discuss media coverage for the Jackson Crusade. In addition he wants to spend some time with Ruth, whom he will not see for about two weeks after he leaves Montreat on Wednesday.

As he describes this impossible-sounding schedule the telephone rings. It is T.W. calling to say that a reporter for the Washington *Post* would like to talk to Billy about the deteriorating situation in Southeast Asia. This gives me the opportunity to inquire about the manner in which Graham communicates to the press.

Obviously if he has something to say on almost any issue he can simply call the wire services with a statement and his views will be immediately transmitted throughout the nation and the world. More often, however, newsmen want to know what he thinks on important public issues, and they will write, call, wire or at times unexpectedly show up at the Montreat office looking for a story. Since almost anything he says is newsworthy, Graham learned a long time ago that he must be circumspect in his handling of the press. He sincerely wants to co-operate with the media and he realizes their need for information and comment, but he also must keep in mind that when he speaks on an issue he represents tens of millions of evangelicals who highly value his views on pressing issues.

Graham must always remember that his basic constituency, while holding theological views similar to his own, is far from monolithic on public matters or on many moral and

ethical questions and he cannot be either too far ahead or
too far behind these masses of followers. The fact is that
over the years he has consistently been ahead of the evangelical community on major issues such as race relations,
ecumenism, war and peace and on the traditionally thorny
questions involved in evangelical Christian life-style. Indeed
it can fairly be stated that Graham has brought evangelicals,
particularly in the United States, into a much broader social
and political context than many would have thought possible twenty-five years ago.

Graham, however, has been careful not to be a crusader
or to take on the self-righteous tone of the do-gooder. His
views on race as well as other public questions are consistently formulated on biblical grounds, and this of course
adds to the force of his opinions. He has been able to communicate to evangelicals a scriptural raison d'être for social
concern and activity. It should also be said that, while
Graham has articulated his views forcefully and with genuine intelligence and at times real courage, he has at the
same time done so with grace and a singular lack of guile or
self-serving posture.

Salaries instead of "love offerings"

Graham also realizes that there are some in the media
who distort his comments and others who would like nothing better than to catch him in inconsistencies or better yet
who yearn to identify him with unethical actions or personal
scandal. Those journalists who over the years of Graham's
public career have harbored these wishes have been totally
frustrated and disappointed. In a world pervaded by greed,
envy and corporate and personal corruption, Graham, who
has been subjected to as close personal and professional
scrutiny as any public figure, has emerged as an incor-
ruptible person. Indeed one of the foundation stones of his
ministry has been the unshakable belief that to fulfill his
mission the evangelist must conduct his activities according
to the highest ethical standards.

Even today, three decades after the initial forming of the

Graham Team, Billy, Grady Wilson and Cliff Barrows still recall the day in Modesto, California, when Billy asked each of his associates to write down what they understood to be the classic public criticisms of evangelism and mass evangelists. (In Jackson, Graham would mention this long-ago session to a large group of young ministers and seminarians and would detail all of the traditional objections to evangelism that he and his colleagues were determined to avoid.)

The first and most important item on the list of criticisms concerned finances. To dispel any notion or possibility of financial wrongdoing or mismanagement Graham, as early as 1950, at the suggestion of late Dr. Jesse Bader of the National Council of Churches, established the non-profit Billy Graham Evangelistic Association as the channel through which the ever-increasing income from his ministry would flow. In addition, he determined that he would no longer receive the "love offering" traditionally given to an evangelist at the conclusion of a series of meetings. Instead Graham and his associates went on salary.

Today Graham earns twenty-five thousand dollars a year, not a princely sum for the head of a fifteen-million-dollar-a-year organization. He also receives income from royalties and fees on books, articles and his newspaper column, but all of these funds are held in trust for his wife and children. Even the gifts from heads of state and other luminaries, ranging from golf clubs to stereos to silver services, which T.W. showed me in the office storage room, are not used by the Grahams. All of this has of course been reported in the press, but there are still writers who periodically investigate Graham's finances in hopes of finding something askew.

Although he has a highly competent press staff, Graham normally deals directly with the media. His staff sets up interviews, particularly in Crusade cities or in places where he has long-standing speaking dates, but in general reporters experienced in dealing with the Graham organization try to get to Billy through T. W. Wilson.

The Washington *Post* journalist evidently fits into this category and I wonder what Billy will say to him when they talk.

Billy Graham and Richard Nixon

Since the topic of news has come up I venture to ask Billy what his relations have been with Mr. Nixon since the President left office. Billy responds that he has talked on the telephone several times with the ex Chief Executive and has visited him once at San Clemente, but other than this he has had little direct contact with the Nixons. He then discusses the last months of the Nixon presidency.

Apparently Mr. Nixon, who has been friendly with Graham since they first met in Washington in 1950, was very angry with an article on Watergate written by Graham for the Op Ed page of the New York *Times*. In any case, Nixon during the last nine months of his presidency did not go out of his way to contact Graham. There is little doubt that Graham was strongly pressured to come out against the Watergate episode, and there is also no question that critics of the President, such as the devoutly evangelical congressional leader Representative John Anderson of Illinois, made it easier for Graham to raise the question of Nixon's complicity in Watergate, but the underlying reason for the New York *Times* piece was Graham's sense of outrage at the violently unethical behavior of high public officials.

Watergate ran counter to Graham's view of government as acting on moral principles, and even his long friendship with the chief of state could not inhibit him from reacting strongly against the Watergate phenomenon.

Graham also told me that he felt deeply hurt and perhaps in a sense betrayed by the language and thought patterning revealed in the presidential tapes. Obviously, Nixon had never shown Graham that side of his personality.

It must be remembered that Graham expressed public support for Nixon in both 1968 and 1972. In a sense, Nixon maneuvered Graham into supportive positions such as the President's appearance at a Graham Crusade in Knoxville, Tennessee, in the spring of 1968. In that situation Graham received a telephone call from Nixon that he was flying from Washington to Key Biscayne and would like to stop off in

Knoxville the next evening to appear at the Crusade. Graham knew enough about U.S. geography to realize that the most direct route from the capital to southern Florida does not run through Tennessee, but how could he refuse a President's request, even during an election year?

Four years later the selection of social gospel-oriented George McGovern by the Democrats made it clearly apparent to Graham's evangelical constituency that as the slogan said, "Nixon's the One!" Nixon carefully played up to evangelicals as his telegram of greeting to the eighty thousand participants in the evangelical youth extravaganza Explo '72 clearly indicated. Not coincidentally, Graham was honorary chairman of the Dallas-based event. Nixon was clearly a manipulative individual and he cunningly used the power and prestige of his office to suggest a close ideological and pragmatic tie with Graham in addition to their well-known personal friendship.

Presidents Eisenhower, Johnson and Ford

Graham, who has been close to Presidents Eisenhower, Johnson and Nixon, will not likely identify closely with another U. S. Chief Executive. He suffered both privately and publicly because of his relationship to Mr. Nixon and he is wise enough not to place himself again in this kind of potentially compromising position.

When I visited with Graham he had just returned from a five-hour meeting with President Ford ("where the President read the Bible and prayed with me"), but in general Graham is determined to keep his relationship with Ford in a low profile. He also remarked to me that Rev. Billy Zeoli of Grand Rapids, Michigan, is a very close personal friend of the Fords and that he thought Zeoli could better serve the spiritual needs of the First Family.

It is interesting to note that when Ford assumed the presidency, Zeoli called Graham and asked his advice on how to deal publicly with his relationship to the new President. Apart from this expression of good common sense by Zeoli, it probably indicates that the Nixon situation has engendered a sense of caution among clergy who have access to the President. Graham was, of course, closely identified in the media as a Nixon intimate, and when the full force of the Watergate storm broke many pundits suggested that Graham himself would lose prestige as a result of Watergate. Some commentators went so far as to foolishly suggest a kind of complicity by the evangelist in the Watergate affair.

It should also be said that, as close as Graham was to Nixon, he was closer to President Lyndon Johnson. He spent many more hours in the White House during the Johnson era than in the Nixon years; he was a very frequent guest at the Johnson ranch; he was with the Johnsons on their last weekend in the Executive Mansion and at Mr. Johnson's pre-determined request, Graham preached the sermon at the late Chief Executive's funeral.

In discussing Mr. Johnson, Billy recalls a conversation he had with the then Chief Executive at the Texan's ranch.

"One day," LBJ said, "you are going to be asked to preach at my funeral. You'll come right here, under this tree, and I'll be buried right there—you'll read the Bible and preach the gospel and I hope you'll tell people about some of the things I tried to do."

White House logs also indicate that during the heyday of the Haldeman-Ehrlichman regime, Graham was a very infrequent visitor to the Oval Office. In that period the evangelist was shut off from major policy decisions or from the opportunity to suggest policy directions to Mr. Nixon. In retrospect, one can only feel that Graham would have served the President and the nation far more nobly than did Haldeman-Ehrlichman and the majority of Nixon's key White House staff members.

The shock of the Nixon tapes

I notice that while Graham discusses the Nixon situation he is generally at ease except during that portion of his commentary that involves the tapes. Graham was shocked not only at the vulgar language employed by Nixon but also by the coarse and sometimes brutal comments Nixon made about public personalities. Beyond this, Graham was deeply troubled by the dearth of ethical attitude and behavior revealed in the tapes. In that sense Graham may be naïve; he may be too trusting, too ready to think favorably about a person without examining underlying motivations and character, and in this area T. W. Wilson and other key associates, as well as Ruth Graham, play important roles in tempering Graham's judgments and helping him to see more clearly the faults and in some cases evil intentions of those with whom he comes in contact.

The tendency to seek the good in a person's make-up contradicts in a sense Graham's basic belief in man's sinful nature and total inability to find forgiveness outside of the sacrifice of Christ. On the other hand, Graham's accepting and basically loving nature has kept him from the intolerant attitudes that characterize much of the evangelical leadership's view of the non-saved world. Ironically, perhaps, Graham's loving nature has made him more successful at winning souls than many of his counterparts who seem overly hardened by the actions of the vast number of their fellow men.

I try to put these thoughts aside as I listen to Graham talk about the need for a Christian presence in the political system. I will hopefully reflect on Graham's complex personality when I have had more of a chance to be with and observe him.

Ruth Graham

It is now twelve-fifteen, and Billy, who has been up since 6 A.M., is ready for lunch. He goes to the kitchen and brings back a tray of sandwiches and a pitcher of iced tea. He tells me that Ruth fixed the lunch before she had to leave for a meeting at the Presbyterian Church.

This is an important occasion for the Grahams, because it is the first time Ruth has gone to a social function since her serious fall at her daughter's home in Milwaukee four months previously. Ruth had undergone extensive medical treatment for head and leg injuries, and Billy had been very concerned about her condition. Thankfully, he tells me Ruth is well on her way to a complete recovery, as her drive down the mountain to the church and its ladies' society meeting indicates.

I look forward to meeting Ruth Graham; she is widely respected throughout the evangelical world and is noted for her intelligence and sophistication. The daughter of medical missionary parents, she was born in China and met Billy when they were both students at Wheaton College in Illinois. Both Grahams have remained close to this excellent school over the years. Billy regarded the late V. Raymond Edman, long-time president of Wheaton, as a valued adviser, and Ruth was recently honored by her alma mater with an honorary doctor's degree.

Harold Lindsell, the scholarly and perceptive editor of *Christianity Today,* who knew and dated Ruth before she met Billy, says,

> "Fifty percent of what Billy is, is due to his wife, Ruth. She is a strong person in his life, a confidant, a critic of a constructive nature, a wise counselor."

Other friends of the Grahams have told me of Ruth's influence on her husband in the areas of literature and art. Many of the books Billy reads are suggested to him by Ruth. In addition to her aesthetic contributions, Ruth, and more particularly her father, L. Nelson Bell, exhibited to Billy the viability of faith within the major denominations. This was a crucial lesson for Graham and enabled him to broaden the scope of his ministry.

Graham's early theological education had been at Bob Jones University and the Florida Bible College at Tampa, where the pervading philosophy interpreted the Christian faith in quite narrow terms. At both schools, and to some degree at Wheaton, also, Graham was taught to be wary of mainline denominational life, which was thought to be rife with liberalism and which was prepared to compromise the gospel to achieve social goals. The dynamic, informed and deeply held faith of Dr. Bell, a dedicated, lifelong member of the Presbyterian Church, made a strong impact upon the maturing Billy Graham. Closer to hand, Graham had the example of Ruth, a strong Christian woman who to this day remains a Presbyterian, thus providing a degree of ecumenicity in a household where the husband is a Southern Baptist.

Is Billy "ecumenical"?

Graham is, of course, not ecumenical in the sense that the National or World Council of Churches is. He cannot in good conscience include liberal Christians in his work, nor can he exclude them from his call of personal redemption and individual commitment to Christ. He is ecumenical in the sense that he will not accept an invitation to hold a citywide Crusade unless the majority of churches and pastors in the locality desire his presence. Unlike previous major evangelists and quite different from many dyed-in-the-wool contemporary fundamentalists, Graham can, and does, make common cause with ministers and members of mainline denominational churches, the main criterion for co-operation always being that the Crusade is aimed at achieving personal salvation through Christ.

Graham's "ecumenicity" is a constant source of discussion and dissension within American evangelical ranks. Divisive personalities such as John R. Rice, Bob Jones, Jr., and Carl McIntire use the issue of Graham's "co-operative evangelism" to attack Graham both professionally and personally. Indeed Graham's most vitriolic critics are to be found not among secularists or liberal churchmen but within the ranks of the fundamentalist-evangelical camp.

At times the scorn heaped upon Graham by these Christians goes far beyond the bounds of common decency or the uncommon grace many of these critical individuals claim to have achieved through faith in Christ. It must also be said that Graham's ecumenical spirit has confused many grassroots Christians who have trouble relating to new trends and currents. I recall a college friend who took a church in Wisconsin and almost lost his pulpit when his first sermon praised Graham's ministry. Sometimes confusion over Graham's activities causes normally intelligent people to act in a ludicrous fashion as in the case of a New England Baptist Church's women's society, which on the occasion of Graham's 1965 Boston Crusade held a prayer meeting to decide whether to pray for Graham.

Criticisms and confusions notwithstanding, there is little doubt that Graham's recognition of the possibility of genuine evangelical faith within the mainline bodies broadened his ministry and its potential outreach. In a sense he, more than any person in twentieth-century America, has made evangelical Christianity the mainstream American religion. Nixon understood this, as do Mr. Ford and a host of other political leaders. Graham has brought evangelicalism back to the position of prominence and influence it occupied in earlier periods of U.S. history. Like Jonathan Edwards, Charles Finney and Dwight Lyman Moody, Graham has made an important impact upon the whole fabric of American life. Graham, however, because of the availability of mass communication, has been able to enjoy a more deepseated and far-reaching influence than the earlier evangelists.

It is also true that the thirty years of Graham's active ministry have coincided with three of the most troublesome and tension-filled decades in the nation's history. It is not that Graham developed a message to suit the times or that he altered his original thrust to gain the attention of a problem-weary populace, but that the society was prepared by its upheavals and uncertainties for the positive, salvation-oriented core of Graham's preaching. This is a lesson that the liberal church leadership apparently still cannot learn.

The timeless message

Graham's basic success is not due to gimmickry, false emotionalism, anti-intellectualism or an appeal to the simplistic and more naïve aspects of man's mind and nature, but is rather due to the timeless quality of his message and to the fact that for many, many people his Crusades provide answers in a world where there seem only to be questions. Graham recognizes the existence of difficult social and moral problems but he believes that these issues can be resolved by resorting to scriptural patterns within the over-all framework of the redemptive work of Christ. He provides, then, that which the liberal churches do not, a foundation (claiming for itself eternal viability and credibility) upon which one may lay and execute plans for the amelioration of wrong and the development of a better world order.

The liberal churchman who rushed to Birmingham, Albany, Georgia, or Selma did so out of genuine compassion and a large measure of guilt for the churches' role in the oppression of blacks in America. This, however, was not enough to resolve the basic human questions implicit in racial tension. Very often the liberal white Christian was all for settling things in the Deep South but resisted attempts at changing the status quo in his northern suburban neighborhood.

Graham approaches the racial situation from the standpoint of the need for changed hearts and personalities, changes that to him can come only through acceptance of Christ. He does not feel guilt for past wrongs—he knows very well that guilt can be a cop-out—instead he offers what he believes to be eternally valid guidelines to meet individual and corporate needs, to help the body as well as the soul, to feed and nourish the whole man.

After talking to a number of black pastors and acute observers of the American racial scene I am convinced that Graham's approach has a greater potential for solid achievement than the guilt-ridden, humanistic program developed by the major denominational and interdenominational church groups. Later I would see the fruits of Graham's activity in the racial area at Jackson.

In evaluating Graham's motivations and accomplishments in the area of social justice one must always bear in mind that Graham by self-description and definition is first and foremost an "evangelist." In a statement issued in early 1973 he commented, "I am convinced that God has called me to be a New Testament evangelist, not an Old Testament prophet! While some may interpret an evangelist to be primarily a social reformer or a political activist, I don't! An evangelist is a proclaimer of the message of God's love and grace in Jesus Christ and the necessity of repentance and faith."

Graham has become the unofficial leader of the world's millions of evangelical Christians. Given his fame, global outreach and unusual gifts of communication, it really could not be otherwise. Yet he has not personally sought this role and he would and does gladly share the position of leadership with other well-known and competent evangelicals. While his prestige is so great that he could have molded almost all of the world's evangelicals into his pattern and included them within the framework of his organization he has chosen to work within the network of existing structures.

Graham is not an empire builder, nor does he desire to establish norms of personal or organizational behavior for his evangelical peers. He has used his influence to bring the several factions of evangelicals together for common, positive purposes. He was the driving force behind the 1966 Berlin Congress on Evangelism; his concern for more widespread evangelical discussion of pressing social issues brought U.S. evangelicals together in 1968 and his suggestions on the need for dialogue between Western and third-world Christians gave birth to the 1974 Lausanne Evangelical Conference.

His ecumenical and irenic approach has done much to clarify evangelical strategy and to better personal relations between believers. This last point is no small matter when one realizes that many evangelicals spend a good part of their time and energy in analyzing and dissecting the faith perspectives of other believers. Although evangelicals talk about evangelizing the world, they often fail to join together in an attempt to accomplish this grandiose goal. The Berlin Congress was the first such session in fifty years, this despite the revolutions and societal convulsions that have shaken the earth during the twentieth century. Graham then sees his role vis-à-vis his evangelical cohorts as that of mediator or, better still, a catalyst who is willing to put his prestige on the line for the sake of co-operation and unity.

A share in the calling

At one o'clock Billy is finishing the remains of a lunch which included a cheese, tomato and lettuce sandwich, an apple and black coffee. This is rather simple fare; apparently food holds no great attraction for Billy. Because he eats out so much Billy prefers very simple meals at home. Often he will wander into the kitchen pantry and heat up a can of pork and beans or wieners. On the road he and T.W. or Grady will order up a meal to their hotel room, and it is amazing that Billy looks so well after years of eating "plastic" hotel food.

Billy reminds me that Don Bailey is due in a few moments from the Atlanta Team office. Don, who is flying in to Asheville, will be picked up by T.W., who will use the twenty or so minutes it takes to drive from the airport to the house for a briefing on what Billy would like prepared for his press conference prior to the opening at Jackson.

While we wait for Don to arrive, I ask Billy how he assembled his staff. The story of Billy's early evangelistic work with Cliff Barrows and George Beverly Shea is well known, but I asked how he chose some of the other key people.

Billy replies that two of his closest aides are old friends, Grady and T. W. Wilson, and that when he began in the past-World War II years to travel extensively he asked Grady to accompany him. Grady was and still is able to break Billy up with a story, while at the same time he is a counselor of great common sense and intuitive wisdom.

Later when Grady was busy with his own burgeoning evangelistic schedule, Billy called upon T.W. to be at his side when away from Montreat.

Other important staff people came with Billy through his association with them in the Youth for Christ movement. Today, of course, there are a number of evangelical organizations that work with young people, but in the World War

II era, Youth for Christ was the most visible and successful group centering its ministry among youth. Graham as a leader of YFC came into contact with many of its city directors and one such person, the energetic and brilliant George Wilson, went from being director of Minneapolis YFC to becoming business manager of the nascent Billy Graham Evangelistic Association.

Today, Graham, a vice-president of Youth for Christ International, still draws from the organizations' professional ranks. His Team director for North America, Sterling Huston, is the former executive head of Rochester, New York, YFC.

What is especially impressive about Graham's staff beyond their competence, all-round abilities and positive and endearing personalities is their longevity with Graham. Most if not all of the original Team could have formed their own groups long ago and probably with significant success, but instead they have chosen to stay with Graham, thus giving up the possibility of a larger public image and greater personal ego satisfaction.

If you ask Cliff Barrows or Bev Shea or Grady or T.W. why he stayed he will tell you it is due to two factors. First, his compatibility with Billy Graham the man. Cliff says that in thirty years he never has had one serious disagreement with Billy; he adds that the Team is like a family, and even a recent addition to the Graham organization, the dynamic and very effective black pastor, E. V. Hill of Los Angeles, talks of the immensely rewarding fellowship of the Graham "family." Second, each of Graham's oldest associates is convinced that Billy is called by God to his ministry. By serving with him they share in the calling.

Cliff, Grady and George Wilson will speak about the need for Billy's work and message, the appropriateness of his activity in this particular day. It is as if each of these highly intelligent and very stable men, once having found vocational meaning and being convinced of the validity of their work, cannot be attracted or tempted to leave Graham lest they thwart the will of God. Yet each man in his own way has informed Billy that when and if he feels their usefulness is at an end they will step aside. They do not court favor nor do they expect that Billy will continue to use them for reasons of sentiment or for old-times' sake. The work is too important to them to be left in non-productive hands.

After observing Graham and his top associates close up, I have come away with the feeling that there is none of the toadying-up to the boss so often prevalent in large corporate enterprises.

Indeed, Graham himself sets the tone for this. He is not interested in flattery or in having his opinions confirmed by his staff. He expects frank discussion, and pity the man who tells Billy Graham what he thinks Graham wants to hear.

The organization is, of course, very large today, a far cry from the days when Billy, Bev Shea, Grady and Cliff and Bonnie Barrows would hop across the country to conduct services in places like Pontiac, Michigan, and Kearney, Nebraska. Billy, of course, cannot stay in close touch with all of his associates—they number over two hundred, and if one includes non-professional staff the figure must be doubled. He is, however, interested in the welfare and morale of his people, and when he hears of special problems or difficulties encountered by someone in the organization he takes a keen and personal interest.

He also keeps in touch with the families of Team members. Howard Jones, the first black associate evangelist to be appointed by Graham, tells of Billy's concern for his son, who wrote to Billy inviting him to speak at his college commencement. Billy could not come, but he sent David a long letter advising him about the ministry in the same fashion that Paul wrote to Timothy.

Another time, Billy asked Mrs. Jones what she was doing while Howard traveled, and she answered that she was involved in a teaching program for retarded children. Billy, who has a tremendous curiosity on almost any subject, particularly those with which he is unfamiliar, told her he would like to discuss the subject with her again. Some months later Mrs. Jones asked Billy to speak at the dedication of a new center for the retarded in Ohio, and Billy, remembering the earlier conversation, agreed to come. Almost every member of the Team has a story similar to this to tell about Billy's personal concern for him or her. Every two years the Team, the organization's board of directors and a number of close friends of the association spend two weeks at a retreat setting, reviewing the organization's activities and renewing and strengthening fellowship.

Getting ready to meet the press

As Billy talks about the Team, Don Bailey and T.W. come into the living room. Bailey is a medium-sized, balding, friendly man, a former journalist who exudes an air of competence. At Jackson I would be impressed by his cool under pressure and his unfailing courtesy toward the press.

Billy motions for Don and T.W. to sit but T.W. explains that he has a deskload of mail to answer and about twenty calls to make. Billy asks Don how plans for the Crusade press coverage are coming along and Bailey replies that all is going smoothly. He explains, mostly for my benefit, that the media coverage in Jackson will be mostly local in nature. The wire services will, of course, pick up anything of national interest but basically he expects only a few out-of-state reporters. On the other hand, there will be very good local and state-wide pick-up, and advance interest in the meetings has already produced significant copy. It is also true, of course, that Jackson, Mississippi, is not one of the hardest places in the world for Billy Graham to be understood or appreciated. The area is rife with evangelicals, and if you consider the geographic axis of the Crusade to include Alabama, Tennessee and Louisiana as well as Mississippi you come up with an astounding number of the already interested if not the converted.

This is the genuine Bible Belt, and Don Bailey will not have to sweat too much about suspicious reporters in search of a juicy Graham lead. Yet Bailey is taking the Jackson sessions as he would a series of meetings in hostile country. This is typical of the Graham people—they do not let down; there is a surety of purpose about them, yet without the aura of the fanatic that often accompanies single-mindedness. Don has been at this for many years. He is a professional who knows what problems to anticipate and he will be prepared for all contingencies.

He also knows that his boss is just about the best in the business when dealing with the media. In a sense Don's chief responsibility, unlike that of many PR men who must create and then sustain a public figure's image, is to execute rather than originate sound public relations. To put it simply, Graham is one of the world's best and most knowledgeable PR men. If there are any types of questions that haven't been asked him in thirty years of dealing with the press, they will have to come from the Venus *Sentinel* or the Pluto *Daily News*. Billy will set the tone, he will make the news; Don's job is to see that it is smoothly and accurately communicated.

Today Don has brought along requests for interviews by local TV, radio and press outlets. In addition, he asks Billy to agree to allow Swedish television to tape an interview as part of a special they are doing on Graham. Billy says fine if it can be fitted into his ever-tightening schedule. Don tells Billy where the press will be seated in the stadium, where the media headquarters will be at the hotel and gives Billy a briefing on the Jackson media scene. Don has already spent two days in Jackson, meeting with media officials, and his associate Arthur Matthews is now in Jackson putting the final touches on the press aspects of the Crusade. Bailey and Matthews can expect that the local morning and evening newspapers will carry front-page stories on the Crusade almost every day, and there will also be several TV appearances by Billy and members of the Team.

"The Hour of Decision"

A few minutes after Don leaves, T.W. appears in the doorway.

"I'm going over to Black Mountain to the radio station. Can I tell them when you'll be over for a taping?" Graham says that he will come by the next morning and adds, "Tell them to be set up for two broadcasts; I want to get ahead of schedule so I can give more time to an article I'm writing."

The radio station T.W. refers to is WFGM, a 50,000 watt outlet which along with WMIT-FM makes up the Blue Ridge Broadcasting Corporation. These stations are an adjunct of the Graham ministry and feature religious programs and inspirational music. The facilities of the stations are used by Graham in his preparation for the "Hour of Decision" broadcast. Once Graham's message is recorded in Black Mountain, the tape is shipped the short distance to Cliff Barrows' studio in Greenville, South Carolina. Cliff and his technical assistant, Johnny Lemon, add music, announcements and a tape of Grady Wilson reading the scripture. The finished broadcast is then sent by special messenger to the Walter Bennett advertising agency in Chicago for release to the network.

Billy takes the "Hour of Decision" very, very seriously. In a genuine sense the program provided the foundation for his national ministry. The idea for the broadcast came from Bennett and his partner, Fred Dienert, and the initial money needed for its capitalization was raised during a Graham appearance in Portland, Oregon.

The program began in 1950. Its name came from Ruth Graham. The "Hour of Decision" has become the most listened to and most successful religious broadcast in America, but one would never have guessed this during those first few weeks when Billy was anxiously trying to find the funds to stay on the air to fill out the initial thirteen-week option. The success of the "Hour of Decision" provided the impetus for the formation of the Billy Graham Evangelistic Association, and even today the broadcast elicits more mail response than any other single aspect of the Graham ministry.

In the early days Graham's radio messages reflected the nation's preoccupation with the real or imagined communist threat. Graham attacked communism and warned that the Soviets were preparing to take over America's vital institutions. As the years went by and the political and social climate changed, Graham turned away from the communist menace and directed his attention to the personal problems engendered by a changing and complex society. Personal sin and salvation through Christ, always at the heart of his message, now became a clarion call to America. At the same time Graham found time to analyze the many movements that attracted the attention of millions of persons during the sixties and early seventies. Race, student restlessness, the various liberation movements, questions of materialism, national life-style and the breakdown of the family were discussed with increasing frequency on the "Hour of Decision." Graham seemed to be citing these issues as symptoms of a greater and deeper personal unrest, and his radio preaching took on greater liberty and clarity.

The broadcast presents serious logistical problems for the constantly traveling Graham, and its weekly schedule means that it is the one unchanging pressure point in an increasingly difficult schedule. In the last few years some of this strain has been relieved by Leighton Ford, Billy's brother-in-law and heir apparent, who takes the responsibility for alternate programs. There are individuals in the Graham organization who feel Billy should not have relinquished full-time control of the show. This does not reflect negatively upon the very gifted Ford. These persons simply feel that the radio broadcast presents Graham with his most comprehensive opportunity to reach and influence the nation. One colleague told me that he wished Billy would drop many of his public appearances to concentrate on the "Hour of Decision" messages. Billy has remarked to me how much these broadcasts mean to him, and I have always been impressed by the preparation that seems to go into each program. There is simply no comparison in terms of clarity, organization and consistency between the "Hour of Decision" and 95 per cent of the hundreds of other religious broadcasts heard regularly on stations throughout the country.

50,000 *letters*

Stephanie Wills comes into the living room and reminds Graham that he must dictate several important letters for the evening mail. He usually writes twenty letters a day and this, of course, is only the top of the iceberg of correspondence related to him and his work. These personally dictated communications cover a range of subjects and are addressed to dignitaries, persons directly involved with particular aspects of his far-flung ministry and on occasion to everyday people who have written him concerning a specific issue or personal problem.

The Billy Graham Evangelistic Association headquarters in Minneapolis receives from forty thousand to fifty thousand letters a week, many of them addressed to Billy. This mail is normally doubled after a national telecast. The bulk of mail includes contributions and is answered by an automated process. Other letters ask Billy's help on a wide range of personal matters. These communications are channeled into ten broad areas of response that have been developed by the association's staff over the course of the years. The letters indicate that Mr. Graham has asked the writer to respond to the sender's question. The Minneapolis office never sends out a letter under Graham's signature that the evangelist has not personally dictated. When Graham is traveling, Stephanie, T. W. Wilson and the Minneapolis headquarters will forward particularly urgent communications to him. Graham also receives thousands of telegrams each year, and on November 2, 1964, an incredible avalanche of sixty thousand telegrams poured into Montreat urging him to endorse the Republican presidential candidate, Barry M. Goldwater.

While Billy works on his correspondence I walk outside and take in the lovely view from the mountaintop. I envy him this retreat far from the noise of the crowd and the everyday world. The Montreat home is in essence a refuge from the press of outside forces and events. Here Billy can truly relax, he can read and study on the screened porch, he can jog each afternoon without encountering interruption or the stares of curious onlookers and he can relax in his small thermal bath and allow the accumulated tensions of weeks on the road to ease away. His nearby neighbors are close friends and associates. T.W. lives just down the hillside, and a mile or so from the house Dr. Calvin Thielman, pastor of the Montreat Presbyterian Church, makes his home.

Outlining the sermon

In addition to preparing "Hour of Decision" messages, Graham is working on outlines for the sermons he will deliver at the Jackson Crusade. He is not exactly starting from scratch—he has spent the better part of three decades preaching and there are few themes or subjects that he has not treated or touched upon. If the Jackson series is typical, he will likely devote individual sermons to the problems of youth, family life, the second coming of Christ and the world crisis. Each message will be of about thirty-five minutes long, a far cry from his early Crusade talks, which sometimes ran over an hour.

Graham's preaching generally reflects an informed, middlebrow perception of reality. He is a keen student of current events, and his talks are liberally sprinkled with quotes from news magazines, best sellers and recognized authorities in various fields. His messages are not political or socially provocative, and some critics have accused him of being "simplistic" in his approach to human problems. I ask Graham how he responds to these charges—isn't he bothered by the suggestion that his preaching lacks depth?

"No, my preaching is based on the proposition that the evangelist must articulate a message capable of reaching as broad a base of people as possible. This message must have a sense of urgency and it must articulate in the clearest terms the basic gospel message of salvation through Christ."

From Graham's perspective there is little purpose in giving a message or talk that does not contain the gospel as its major thread. It is true that Graham occasionally speaks before groups that do not expect or welcome a Crusade-type message, but even in these situations Graham quotes scripture and articulates a personal testimony of what faith in Christ means to him. Even if he does not conclude with an invitation, he has in New Testament terminology "sown the seed" and fulfilled his calling as an evangelist to proclaim the good news of salvation.

Graham is troubled by the fact that there are few outstanding preachers active today. He tells me that the same five or six persons are asked to speak at most major church conferences. "When Bishop Arthur Moore [a leading Methodist] was alive he was in great demand, but today there are few men who can preach the way he did."

Graham's messages are not likely to be remembered for their technical competence—the sermons of Bishop James A. Pike and theologian Reinhold Niebuhr exhibit far better construction—but Graham's messages, if only because of the incredible effect they have on diverse types of audiences, are worthy of careful study by seminarians, pastors and other professional church workers whose tasks include preaching.

Careful student

Graham also likes to take advantage of the proximity of Anderson-Montreat College and he will invite a dozen or so students to come up to the house for an evening of intense and lively discussion. Billy serves on the board of the college and in recent years has addressed the entire student body on several occasions. The evangelist has long been interested in education and student life. He feels a certain lack of formal training—he never went beyond the B.A., although he did take some graduate courses in anthropology at the University of Chicago. Interestingly, for a man who has preached to more persons than any other human, he does not hold a degree in theology.

Harold Lindsell sees a virtue in Graham's lack of formal theological education. Lindsell, who has taught at several seminaries, feels that the seminary experience can sometimes dull a man's evangelistic zeal and lessen his sense of priority concerning the necessity for spreading the gospel message. He argues that the great nineteenth- and twentieth-century American evangelists did not have systematic

Singing for the Lord

CRUSADE IN JACKSON

With Norman Sanders,
Crusade associate

The rains wouldn't stop him

(From left)
Don Bailey, George Wilson

(From left)
Charles Riggs, Grady Wilson

(From left)
Joan Tatum, T. W. Wilson

George Beverly Shea

Howard Jones
and daughter

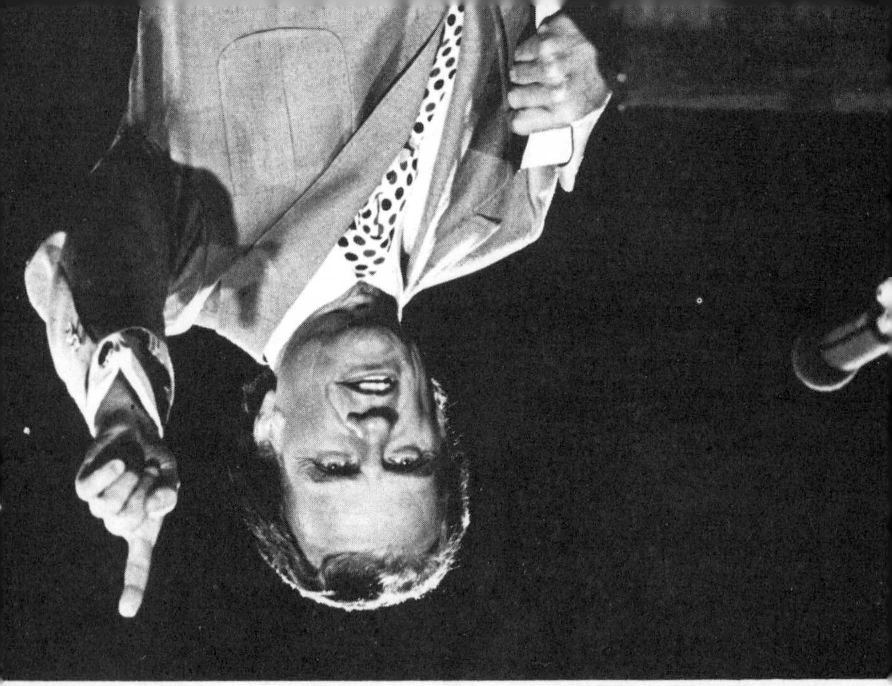

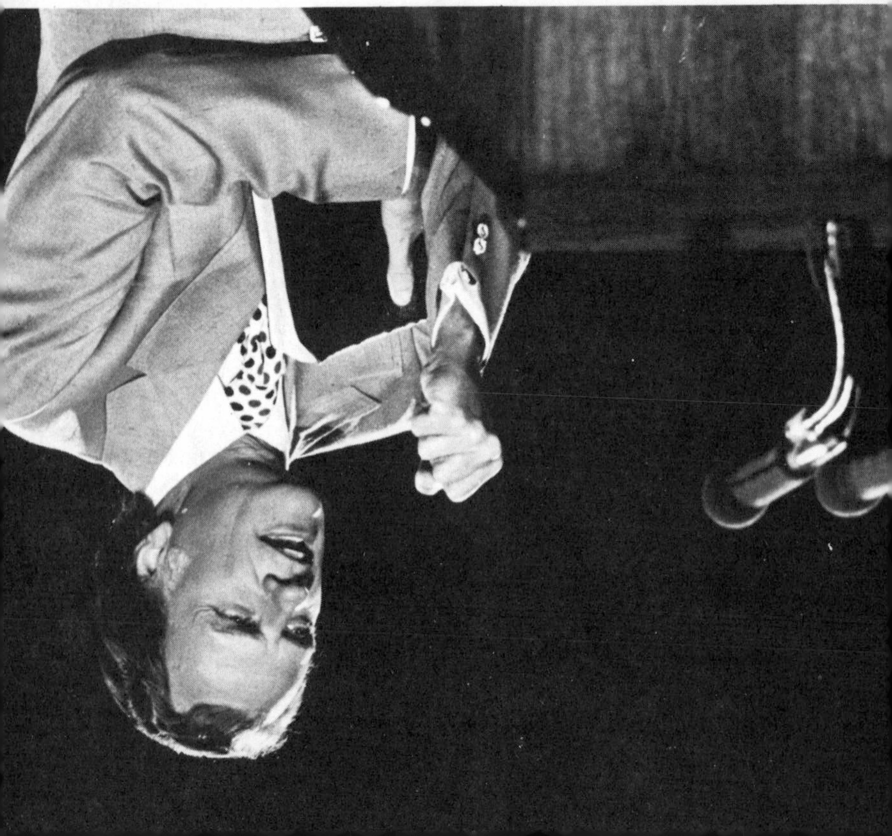

theological backgrounds. Lindsell adds however that Graham is a keen and careful student who over the years has supplemented his Bible education with a wide range of critical readings. Graham also has the gift of extracting information from informed people. He is a great questioner who is able to get to the core of a problem or issue and he seldom forgets what he has learned. At one point in our conversation he asked about our mutual interest in writing, and before long he had me talking at great length and in considerable detail about my work habits, and the pros and cons of literary representation. Billy does not have an agent; in his dealings with his publisher he is represented by a New York attorney, and he also leans heavily upon the advice of his long-time associates Fred Dienert and George Wilson.

Billy has great regard for the value of higher education. A significant portion of his yearly tithe goes to Christian colleges and seminaries, and he takes an active interest in the affairs of several of these institutions.

As he noted, his early educational experiences were undertaken in the shallow and narrow settings of Bob Jones College and the Florida Bible Institute. Yet the years spent at these institutions were of some instructional value. At Bob Jones, Graham learned the dangers of an ultra-fundamentalist world view that shut off the possibility of Christian charity and limited the horizons of one's ministry. At Tampa, Graham deepened his spiritual life, and it was here that he began the systematic study of scripture that would remain an unchanging portion of his daily routine. Here also he evidenced the powers of preaching that would take him from the Florida swamps and backwoods churches to every world continent and capital. It was only when he went up to Wheaton College that Graham came into contact with believers who were prepared to submit to a thoroughgoing intellectual discipline without fear of losing or compromising their faith.

At Wheaton, Billy was known as a man with a tremendous interest in soul winning. One friend recalls seeing him in the mornings, his eyes red from lack of sleep, his expression bearing evidence of hours spent in Bible reading and prayer. Billy also preached in the Wheaton area, first at the Tabernacle Church and then at the Baptist church in Western Springs.

Even today Billy likes to visit Wheaton, and in a few weeks he is to return to the campus for an especially happy occasion, the awarding of an honorary doctorate to Ruth, who is also an alumna of the Illinois school. Recently Wheaton announced the formation of a Billy Graham Evangelism Center.

The center, which will open in 1977, will contain Graham's personal archives, as well as pertinent documentary materials of the Graham Association. In addition, the center will conduct Bible training for laymen and will sponsor an Institute of Evangelism for full-time Christian workers.

Long-distance calls

When I come back into the living room Stephanie is gone and Billy is on the phone. Graham spends a good part of each day on the telephone. Many of the calls put him in touch with the various offices of his world-wide organization. There are currently ten such offices outside the United States ranging from Sydney to Buenos Aires.

In addition, he speaks at least once and sometimes two and three times a day with his Minneapolis headquarters. Most of these calls are initiated by Graham. His staff realizes the complexity of his schedule, and staff members will try to telephone him only on the most urgent matters.

At the same time he receives hundreds of long-distance calls each day at the various Graham offices. A number of these calls are from distraught persons who want to share a personal problem with the evangelist. On the day I visit him a call is taken in Minneapolis from a woman whose husband has been in an automobile accident and who asks that Billy visit him in the hospital. Later that day the deputy foreign minister of Taiwan calls concerning Graham's upcoming

Taipei Crusade. Graham's Montreat office maintains a twenty-four-hour switchboard and all calls are screened, so that only those people who should reach him do so. If this process was not in effect, Graham would be totally swamped by telephone calls.

George Wilson

The call Billy is currently involved with is to George Wilson, the executive vice-president of the Billy Graham Evangelistic Association. Wilson, a small but compact sixtyish native of North Dakota, has been with Graham since 1944. From 1947 to 1950 he served as the business manager of Northwestern Schools, a Minneapolis Bible college Graham headed. In 1950, when the "Hour of Decision" first went on the air, Wilson got a call from Graham asking him to set up an entity that would handle the funds needed to sustain the program. Graham told Wilson to rent a small office and to borrow some furniture and office machines, because "we might not be on the air more than thirteen weeks." Operating from a cramped six-hundred-square-foot space, Wilson set about to organize what has become one of the most efficiently run religious operations in the world. Looking back, Wilson told me, "I think I would have been scared to death if I'd have known it was going to develop to the extent it has."

At first glance Minneapolis did not seem to be a very propitious setting for a national headquarters, particularly because Billy and the majority of the Team members lived in the South, but with the advent of *Decision* magazine about fifteen years ago, the Minneapolis site, less than one hundred miles from some of the world's largest paper mills, seemed almost providential. Today the magazine appears in four English-language editions and six other foreign-language versions including Spanish, Chinese and Japanese, as well as Braille, using 300 to 400 tons of paper a month. In addition, the association needs another million pounds of paper every time a Crusade is telecast or a book is published by its World Wide Books subsidiary.

Business-like operation

Wilson describes the BGEA as "business-like but not op-erating like a business." A few years ago a group of manage-ment experts toured the Graham Minneapolis headquarters and were surprised by the constant flurry of activity. One of them remarked to Wilson, "My, all of these people are actu-ally working." Wilson replied that all the workers in the office had a special motivation that led them to putting in a sixty-minute hour.

In his tenure as chief of the Graham business operations, Wilson has been innovative and highly successful. Recently an auditing firm discovered that the BGEA's overhead runs to about 6½ per cent, an amazingly low figure and less than the 8 per cent overhead of the National Red Cross, widely considered the most cost effective non-profit organization in the United States.

Nevertheless, the Graham organization operates on a first-class basis. The Minneapolis facilities are modern and house all of the latest available office and mailing equipment; and the motion picture studio at Burbank, California, could rival the facilities of many secular film companies. Wilson and his colleagues are not afraid to change their pattern of opera-tion if a more efficient and cost-saving approach is feasible.

For years World Wide Pictures, the Graham film sub-sidiary, distributed its films through traveling repre-sentatives who would take a film to a local church, project it and then receive a goodwill offering from the congregation. Wilson determined that considerable savings could be ac-complished in salary, travel and living costs if the films were distributed on a rental basis. Today World Wide Pictures has five distribution points around the United States and most of the contact between the company and churches is done through the mail or by telephone. This change in sys-tem also allowed the company to have better control over its prints and to drop the need to purchase costly projection machinery.

One of Wilson's latest changes has been to initiate a

miniaturizing system for the five million names on the *Decision* magazine mailing list. Under this system, forty to fifty women, working in their homes, type the list on sheets of special paper. These lists are then read in seconds by an automatic scanner and are placed on a magnetic tape. Once a week the tape is photographed and 150,000 names along with other pertinent information are put on 4×6-inch plastic Microfiche cards.

The introduction of miniaturizing is consistent with Wilson's credo that "any business becomes strong through common sense, wise planning and keeping abreast of current facts."

The Graham organization works on a very strict budget; Graham, who is involved in every major policy decision, does not believe in deficit financing. He feels a tremendous sense of responsibility to and trust in the multitudes of people who have contributed money, and he will not allow funds to be wasted or spent in frivolous or potentially nonproductive ways. One of his close associates told me, "Billy is an evangelist first but he is also one of the best businessmen I know."

The BGEA has a strong twenty-six-member board of directors, which meets four times a year. In between board sessions the organization is directed by an executive committee, which meets at least once each month. Two years ago, the board, which consists mainly of successful business people, took on its first two blacks, Rev. Edward Hill of Mount Zion Baptist Church, Los Angeles, and Dr. John Williams, a pastor from Kansas City, Missouri. More recently the board welcomed its first woman member, Mrs. Mary Crowley of Dallas, Texas. Every two years the board and the world-wide Graham staff go on a two-week retreat for a time of reporting and fellowship.

Financing of a telecast

This afternoon Graham and Wilson are talking about the mail response to a just completed television series. It costs $250,000 to finance one nationwide telecast, and it is becoming increasingly more difficult to raise this kind of money, despite the fact that the average gift to the BGEA has gone up from $5 in 1973 to $8 in 1974. The long-term inflationary spiral has made the fund-raising dollar harder to come by and then less useful when it is finally brought in. Last year Graham sent out a special letter asking long-time contributors to give more.

Yet, the problem of finding the funds to support his ministry does not appear to give Graham real uneasiness, nor does it limit his creativity and inventiveness. George Wilson attributes this lack of anxiety to Graham's attitude of faith. As he told me in Jackson, "Every so often Billy comes up with programs that just don't seem feasible, but you see the hand of the Lord in it—you know that whatever program he is going to project the Lord has led him to it in the hours of the night."

Indeed, one of the most arresting aspects of Graham's personality is his capacity to think big, to attempt programs that others would not see as feasible or possible. The launching of the "Hour of Decision" radio broadcast, the introduction of televised Crusades, the initiation of *Decision* magazine, which today boasts a circulation of five and a half million, the development of a major film ministry were actions that men of lesser vision, drive or perhaps faith would have been reluctant to attempt. Graham is not only the best known and most successful evangelist of his time but he has built a viable organization that will very likely continue as an important force on the world religious scene long after he retires or dies. Billy is very conscious of his role as the head of the association. He does not shy away from the responsibilities of this post, and in a sense he relishes the daily challenges his leadership role presents.

As he hangs up the receiver, Billy tells me of his great affection and respect for George Wilson. "It is so helpful to have someone like George in charge of the business side of my activities. He is reliable, has great integrity and he walks with God."

On a lighter note, Graham then tells me of the time he called Wilson at home from Frankfurt, Germany. "When

George answered he sounded sleepy," Billy recalls. "I asked him why he was so groggy, and he replied 'You would be tired too if someone called you at four o'clock in the morning.' It seems I did not take into account the six-hour time difference between Frankfurt and Minneapolis when I made the call."

"The Hiding Place"

Billy is interrupted by the ring of the telephone. It is T.W. calling to say the latest rushes of the World Wide Pictures film, *The Hiding Place*, are ready for viewing in the office projection room.

The Hiding Place is the most ambitious film project yet undertaken by the Graham organization. It is capitalized at close to two million dollars and marks the first time that the Graham film subsidiary has employed several major Hollywood performers. The project is very close to Graham's heart.

Based on the best-selling book of the same name, *The Hiding Place* relates the dramatic experiences of Corrie Ten Boom and her family during World War II.

Corrie's home in the Netherlands city of Haarlem was used as a refuge for hundreds of Jews seeking escape from Hitler's extermination campaign. Eventually the Ten Booms' activities were discovered and Corrie and her sister, Betsie, were sent to the infamous Ravensbrück concentration camp. Betsie died in the camp, but only one week before all of the women in her barracks were put to death, Corrie was released as a result of a clerical error.

She emerged from the camp with deep faith, a faith that was able to sustain her during the agony of Ravensbrück. In the days following her release she recalled a dream Betsie had shortly before her death. In the dream the two sisters go out into the world to tell of their faith, which could bring victory over hate, fear and discouragement. At the heart of this desire to spread their beliefs was Betsie's conviction that "there is no pit so deep and no darkness so black that the love of God cannot triumph over it."

As we drive down the mountain to the office, Graham tells me about Corrie's current activities. She has a world-wide speaking ministry, heads a foundation, publishes a monthly magazine and is much in demand by young people as a counselor and adviser. All of this activity is only slightly less than amazing when you consider that Corrie is eighty-four years old.

Billy and Corrie have been friends for many years. She often appears at Crusade meetings and has been a frequent guest in the Graham home.

I ask Billy why he has put so much effort and resources into *The Hiding Place* film. He says that the theme of Christians helping Jews in a period of crisis is very timely, given the current world situation.

"I am worried about the status of the Jews. The oil situation and attacks on the Judaeo-Christian tradition are signs that things could go badly for the Jewish people. I hope this film will remind Christians of their responsibility toward the Jews."

Graham seems to echo the words of Corrie's father, who, when questioned by his pastor as to why he risked his safety and the security of the family for the Jews, replied, "It will be an honor for me to give my life for God's ancient people."

When we reach the screening room, T.W. is there, and he briefs Billy on the status of the production. The film is almost finished, a rough cut will be ready in about three weeks and some important decisions have to be made concerning the production's length and final scenes. This afternoon Billy will see a suggested close that features Corrie as she is today, sitting in the old Ten Boom house in Haarlem.

A few people on the World Wide Pictures staff believe the film should end with a freeze shot of Jennifer Cliff, who plays Corrie, leaving the Ravensbrück camp. Billy leans toward the real-life Corrie ending, and what he sees in these rushes confirms this view in his mind. When the lights go up he picks up the phone and places a call to Bill Brown, a long-time Team member and currently president of World Wide Pictures. Brown, who has just returned to the company's Burbank, California, studios from London, where the film's interiors were shot, is busy planning a series of previews in key cities throughout the United States. Graham informs Brown that the scenes he has just watched are very good, and he would like the film to close with these shots.

Brown asks the boss if he is satisfied with the length. The film runs a little over two and a half hours, while most features in commercial distribution run from an hour and fifty minutes to two hours. Theater operators prefer a two-hour film. This gives them the opportunity to have one extra showing during the course of a normal day.

Graham, however, is reluctant to make any cuts. He has been involved with films long enough to realize the Herculean efforts that would be required to cut a half hour from this film, and he earnestly feels that the message would be diluted if the film were significantly changed. The issue is open to several interpretations and potential solutions, but Graham has made a decision and this settles the matter.

I am struck by his familiarity with the nomenclature of the motion picture industry and his grasp of both the technical and artistic aspects of film making. As a top-flight businessman he also is aware of the monetary realities involved in distribution, theater rentals, ticket pricing and promotion. There is no doubt that the Graham organization will go all out to make *The Hiding Place* a success—everyone that I talk to in the association believes in the project and is carried along by Graham's enthusiasm and direction. This film is a far cry from *Mr. Texas,* the first Graham cinematic attempt, which was budgeted at $50,000.

His habit of hard work

As I observe Graham I am deeply impressed by his capacity for hard work. As a boy growing up on a dairy farm he had to pull his weight by completing a daily routine of dull and difficult chores, and this early activity apparently established a lifetime pattern. During his high school years he worked summers as a Fuller Brush salesman, and he was regarded as one of the best workers in the North Carolina region. At the Florida Bible Institute he washed dishes, and at Wheaton he and a friend moved furniture to earn spending money. At Wheaton he also devoted hours to Bible study, meditation and prayer, and some of his friends wondered where he found the time also to preach and to court Ruth Bell. For the last thirty years he has conducted a schedule that would tax to the limit the energies of most men, yet he is as busy today as he ever was and he shows no sign of a desire to let up and rest on his considerable accomplishments.

Harold Lindsell, who has been a friend and confidant of Graham's for many years, says that "Billy would go crazy if he had to sit still for two weeks. If he went to a cloister it would cease to be a cloister; it would become a beehive."

Graham is filled with nervous energy. His mind seems to race about, eager to absorb and catalogue various pieces of information concerning his organization and the outside world. He is a notoriously poor sleeper, and perhaps the only limitation on his almost relentless work drive is his serious and chronic struggle with high blood pressure. Everyone around him urges him to slow down, to cut his schedule to make more time for golf and other forms of recreation, but Graham is driven by a sense of responsibility, first to the numberless persons who do not share his spiritual world view, and then to the organization he has built and to the persons who work for him. It is as if at this stage in his life he is boxed in, a pattern has been formed that cannot be changed, the momentum is too great, the responsibilities of leadership too well defined. I ask him if he has given any thought lately to retirement, as it is enjoyed by many men in their late fifties who have led far less enervating a life. Billy responds that he has no plans to retire. "I see the needs of the world as being so great," he says, "the workers so few and fragmented. Yet, I also believe we are on the verge of a major spiritual breakthrough and I want to share in this movement of God in history."

Graham also seems to be one of those for whom work is a tonic. He appears to derive great satisfaction from his work. As I watch him talk on the telephone or chat with Stephanie and T.W. or look through a batch of mail there is a zestfulness about him—he gives me the impression that nothing is routine, everything is of genuine interest.

When I ask him about this he replies that he regards each new day as a challenge, an opportunity to serve God and to add to the building of his kingdom. There is also an air of optimism about Graham. Surely he must have his moments of depression but just as surely he must bounce back. There is a maturity to his faith that enables him to perceive the ugly side of human existence while believing in the ultimate wisdom of God's plan for mankind.

Women's Lib?

The afternoon light is fading when we leave the office. T. W. Wilson walks us to Billy's car. He will come back to the house later in the evening and drive me to my hotel in town. The ride up the mountain is quiet; Graham is obviously thinking of the rushes he has just viewed or perhaps he is simply enjoying the gorgeous scenery of the mountainside. I break into his thoughts and ask what is on his agenda for the remainder of the day. He replies that from here on the schedule is flexible—we will have dinner, he may make a few calls, there will be time for conversation.

When we reach the house Ruth is busy preparing Billy's favorite meal. She enjoys working in the kitchen. Beatrice Long, her maid for twenty-five years, is retired and comes in only a few days a week. The Grahams also employ George and Corrine Burgin, who perform a number of necessary duties in a household where one or both of the residents are often away.

Billy is quite proud of Ruth and rightly so. In 1943 her Wheaton College housemother described Ruth as, "Very attractive, beautiful to look at and excellent taste in dress. The most beautiful Christian character of any young person I have ever known. And she has the intellectual qualities to make a success in any work she would choose to undertake."

In her adult life Ruth has developed into a singularly well-rounded and mature person. She has been a great help to her husband and she has also emerged as a Christian leader in her own right. Ruth is respected by women around the world and she is a favored speaker at many women's gatherings and functions. In recent years, since the children have married and started their own homes, she has been free to travel extensively with Billy, and later in the year she will join her husband on his swing through Asia.

Billy goes to the fireplace and places some logs in the already roaring fire. He sits in an easy chair and tells me that Ruth has been giving increasing attention to the right-to-life question. She serves as one of the organizers of a task force aimed at mobilizing Protestant women "in defense of life" and she will host a conference on the subject at Montreat during the summer.

I ask Graham his views on women's liberation. He is very emphatic in stating his belief that women should have equality of opportunity but he also thinks the women's movement may be fostering a confusion in male-female roles.

"I think a woman ought to be proud to be a woman and a man ought to be proud to be a man. The man must always remember that his wife is not an object but a person."

I suggest that some feminists feel that organized religion is oppressive in terms of its teaching and practices, but Billy takes issue with this premise.

"If you go into areas of the world where Christianity is not important or Judaism has never gone, you'll find the woman in a very inferior position. What is more," Graham adds, "the Judaeo-Christian tradition has formulated the best basis I know for relationships between the sexes. The Bible teaches each mate respect for the other and establishes principles which lead to happy and productive family living."

Dinner and an after-dinner walk

Ruth calls us to dinner. She has baked potatoes in a wood stove and has broiled steaks on top of the ashes. The meal is accompanied by a tossed salad and coffee. The Grahams talk about the activities of their children, an upcoming trip, the need for Billy to replace an aging jacket and the possibility of riding over to Charlotte tomorrow to have lunch with the Grady Wilsons. The conversation is similar in form to that being conducted in homes all over the nation. The Grahams are very much at ease with one another and they are used to having guests at their table. There is not the slightest evidence of pretension or self-importance, and the normality of the evening is broken only by the ring of the telephone: it is the White House calling to confirm Dr. Graham's upcoming appointment with the President. (Later I will learn that the two men spent five hours together praying, reading the scripture and discussing a wide range of current issues.)

Graham asks if I would like to walk along the hillside, and we go out for a stroll. The air is clear and clean, a pleasant change from the polluted atmosphere of New York. The first stars of evening are making their appearance and they seem so close as to be within touching range. Out here even in the company of a world-famous person I feel especially small and inconsequential, and my thoughts run in the direction of the spiritual. . . . I ask Graham why he believes the end of the world is at hand; I have heard him speak on this theme on the "Hour of Decision" and in telecasts, but are events really coming to a head? "Well, it's, of course, foolish to fix dates," he replies. "Jesus warned against it, medieval literature is filled with doomsday prophecies, Luther said he might live to see the end of his age, John Wesley expected the final overthrow of the beast in 1836. But I do believe we are living in the last days and that we've been living in the last days for a long time.

"I'm convinced we're moving toward that final day, the climactic moment when Christ will come and set up a new world and the kingdom of God will prevail."

His position on the second coming of Christ has not led him into an exaggerated pietism or to a total sense of hopelessness as to what can be accomplished on the spiritual, moral and social levels.

Graham will continue to preach and direct his organization, armed with the conviction that in the proper moment the eternal plan of God will be fulfilled.

He is however very emphatic about the ultimate victory God will achieve.

"And all the evil systems of this world, all the lying, cheating, hating, injustice and corruption are going to come to an end. But they cannot come to an end through any form of government the world has ever known. Every type of government has been permeated with corruption, evil and greed, but there's one type we have not tried. That is theocracy, with Christ on the throne and the nations of the world confessing him. Then, and only then, can the world be free of the bondage of sin and be set free, to have peace, because he is the Prince of peace. And I feel this about America. I love America, but I am not an ambassador for America. I represent a higher power. I am an ambassador for Christ, and someday his flag will wave over every nation of the world."

Our discussion moves into a lighter vein. Billy tells me how happy he is to be at home and how much he looks forward to the time when he can spend months, rather than days or weeks, at Montreat. I ask what activities would occupy him under a more relaxed regimen. He says he would like to devote more time to study, to writing, and he would also like to teach at a seminary or university. The conversation has the character of wishful thinking—we both know that his schedule for the next eighteen months is totally filled, and I think back to what Cliff Barrows said to me. "I don't imagine the time will ever come when Billy will say, 'Well, the hay is in the barn and I can sit back and relax.'"

It is getting downright chilly, and we return to the house. Graham spends the next hour working on the manuscript of his book about angels. He started the project the previous Christmas, and last week he made a major breakthrough by dictating the final chapter in two hours, a task that ordinarily would require two weeks of his very valuable time.

I ask how he became interested in doing an entire book on such an esoteric subject?

"When I started to research the subject, I found that very

little had been written on angels. There are a lot of books on demons and devils and the occult, and you'd almost think the devil is going to win the whole thing. But God has principalities and powers at his command, and they are at the disposal of Christians, and they are going to come with drawn swords and flaming chariots and are going to win the battle against the devil and his forces."

At ten, Billy emerges from his study and he and Ruth sit together on a small couch watching a TV detective thriller. Billy is not a television fan, even though he does like to watch news and documentary programs. More often than not he will relax with a book or a recording, but television does act as a mild and at times welcome distraction, and it is a pastime the Grahams can enjoy together.

Ruth and Billy sit holding hands, their deep mutual affection and love clearly visible. They have come a long way since their first date on a snowy Wheaton Sunday when they went to a recital of Handel's *Messiah*, so many great and unexpected experiences have filled the intervening years; and in all the days they have shared and the months they have been apart they have by act and example immeasurably contributed to the well-being of multitudes of people, and one senses they have many miles more to go before they sleep. Just as the TV mystery reaches its denouement, T.W. comes into the room and I make my good-bys.

Just being himself

It is doubtful that Graham, unlike many middle-aged men, has ever undergone an identity crisis. Although I am certain that he is constantly amazed at his popularity, station in life and enormous influence, he seems assured that he is fulfilling God's will for his life and that his actions are guided by the Holy Spirit. In his introspective moments he must also know that he has been gifted in ways distinctive to the ministry he has chosen for his life's work.

He is a charismatic personality of the first rank. If you walk into a room where he is located you are immediately aware of his presence. A magnetism radiates from him, and

it is easy to be swept up in the aura of good feeling and success that surrounds him. He has an excellent voice, and his
rich southern accent makes his words sound warm and ap-
pealing. He is tall, slim and handsome, and his smile and
pleasant demeanor are contagious. It is as if he was uniquely
fitted out to perform the role he has been handed, and one
could almost suspect that he has been packaged by Madison
Avenue or Hollywood.

I say "almost," because his unique quality is his trans-
parency. He is like a pane of glass—you can look through
him. He is direct and open and exhibits a singular lack of os-
tentation. He is almost too good to be real, but the incredible fact is that he is real, and all of the fame and success
have not jaded him or made him cynical or changed him in
any negative way. He has remained sensitive to people and
their needs. He is able to identify with others; he talks to a
person, never at a person.

I well recall a meeting held in 1969 between Graham and
a group of rabbis and Jewish officials. The session came at
the end of his Madison Square Garden Crusade. Many of
the Jewish participants were very skeptical of Graham and
his methods and motivation, and several were rather unim-
pressed by the Graham they viewed on television. After an
hour and a half of questions, comments and coffee, Graham
had become a friend of every man in the room. There were
no gimmicks involved; Graham was just being himself. Over
the years I have heard many such stories from Graham's associates and occasionally from his detractors and former
enemies.

Three reasons for his prominence

Despite Graham's natural gifts and, as he would quickly
say, the providence and sovereignty of God, there are logical explanations as to why he came to prominence in the immediate postwar period.

First, he was allied with the vibrant and highly successful
and visible Youth for Christ movement. Billy served as the
organization's vice-president, and most of his early travels

were on behalf of YFC. From the ranks of Youth for Christ he found a number of highly motivated and capable men who would form the nucleus of his organization. His Youth for Christ ministry also put him in touch with the international evangelical movement and made his name known to a broad-based segment of American and European Christians.

Second, his national ministry began at the moment that liberal Christianity was fading. The horror of World War II and the demonic forces it had unleashed upon the world all but negated the optimism and bringing of the kingdom of God on earth philosophy that had so permeated much of main-line denominational Protestantism in the first half of the twentieth century. To anyone but the most Pollyannish observer, the world instead of getting better was worse than it had ever been. The fundamentalists (as evangelicals preferred to be called in those days) after suffering ignominy and scorn as a result of the fundamentalist-modernist controversy of the 1920s and the Scopes Trial now seemed justified in viewing society as unredeemable without the special action of God.

Third, the growing complexity of society, the displacements caused by the war and the sweeping changes in behavior and life-styles, coupled with deepening anxiety over a nuclear confrontation and the apparent sinister communist plot to undermine morality and traditional American values, led many persons to seek out a personalized religious experience that would provide a shelter against the onslaughts of a cruel and indifferent world.

Graham thus came on the national scene at a propitious moment, as if fulfilling that view of history which sees a man coming to prominence at a given time, whereas in another age it might never have happened.

Keeping up with the children

Stephanie Wills hands Billy several drafts of his "My Answer" syndicated newspaper column. The column appears in over three hundred newspapers and has an unvarying format with Billy answering a question sent in by readers. Because of his many other commitments and the considerable time spent away from his office and study, Billy has normally received suggestions and drafts for the columns from his aides Lee Fisher, John Akers and Dr. Robert Featherstone. Each draft however is carefully edited by Graham, and each column bears his indelible stamp. He has also written hundreds of columns himself on subjects especially of interest to him.

Today Graham looks over questions and answers dealing with alcoholism, disobedient children and the problems of aging. Billy is particularly concerned with the apparent disintegration of the American family. Many of his sermons have dealt with the problems of family living, and he tries to encourage family-wide attendance at his Crusades.

Billy was brought up in a warm but strict atmosphere—his parents provided a secure setting for his childhood, and Graham describes his mother and father in proud and loving terms. Graham is also aware that his own children have had to grow up without the constant presence of a father. Ruth has had to fulfill both parental roles for inordinately lengthy periods of time. Some months ago the Grahams' oldest child, Bunny, commented to *Good Housekeeping* on Ruth's contributions to her husband's work. "Without her, Daddy could never had done what he's done. Just imagine if he had a wife nagging him on the phone every night saying, why aren't you home or the water pipes just burst." Bunny added that she "never heard a cross word" uttered between her parents.

Billy and Ruth have tried to keep up with the changing tastes and fads that their children, like all growing youngsters, have been affected by. During their children's teen years, Billy and Ruth subscribed to a magazine that published the lyrics to the songs that blared away from their rooms. Billy stays in regular touch with his five children, who are scattered about in several parts of the country. He will sometimes stop off to see one or another on a business trip. When he goes to Montreal later in the year he will stop en route and spend a day with Gigi and her husband, Fred

Dienert. During the Thanksgiving and Christmas holidays
the children and the Grahams' eleven grandchildren will
come to Montreat for a family reunion. Billy and Ruth have
made a very conscious effort to provide a biblical nexus for
their home life.

The need to preach simply

Graham is a great student of the Bible and he is familiar
with all of its themes and currents. He cannot, however,
preach on many aspects of the scripture because as an evangelist his ministry is principally one of reductionism. This
does not mean that his preaching and approach are simplistic—rather he must take the New Testament account of
Jesus' life and substitutionary death and make this the core
of his message. He must be able to reach the average man
clearly and succinctly but with intense feeling and verve.
His sermons are not meant for the seminary lecture hall or
gatherings of long-time believers. His mission is to proclaim
the gospel in as simple, relevant and forceful a manner as
possible.

In a sense, this is frustrating for him, because, as he tells
me, he would love to preach on many different biblical subjects. For instance, he would like to give a series of talks on
specific themes, but this is not the way of the evangelist.
From my point of view, the great virtue in Graham's con-
tinuous systematic study of the Bible is the assurance and
authority it gives to his preaching.

The Bible is the *sine qua non* of his ministry, his foundation stone, compass and focal point. Yet he does not fall into
the trap that reaches out to snare so many well-meaning
evangelicals. He is not a Biblicist, he does not limit the ex-
periential world to the Bible, nor does he use the scripture
as some kind of magic-like entity. He truly believes the
Bible to be the inspired word of God, but he knows that unless activated by a man's life the teachings of scripture can
be detached and meaningless to a world that looks to a person's deeds for proof of one's words.

Reading and writing of books

As we talk, I notice a copy of a recently published book, *Eleanor: The Years Alone* on the coffee table and I ask Billy about his reading habits. He replies that he usually does not read books all the way through. Ruth, or perhaps a staff member or friend, will suggest a book to Graham and quite often she marks or dog-ears the portions she thinks will be of particular interest to him. He has just completed *Jaws* and the *Gulag Archipelago*. He also reads the New York *Times* and Washington *Post* on a daily basis.

When he mentions the *Gulag* he tells me of his meeting with Alexander Solzhenitsyn. Graham was approached by an intermediary who told him that the Nobel Prize-winning author wanted to see him. A week later, Graham, who had business to conduct in Europe, flew to Stockholm and spent two hours with the Russian exile. Solzhenitsyn wanted to know about religious conditions in the United States and other world areas, and Graham was most anxious to ask about the status of religion in the Soviet Union. The session with the Russian author is not unusual. Graham is often approached by major personalities and celebrities who want to talk with him or share a particular problem or concern. He has been received by scores of heads of state, and many of these leaders see him as having a prophetic voice even if they disagree with his Christian standpoint. U.S. politicians are very interested in being seen with Billy and in cultivating him. In the presidential election year of 1972, Graham attended the ground breaking for the Lyndon Johnson library in Texas, and several would-be Democratic candidates, including Hubert Humphrey, Henry Jackson and George McGovern, studiously sought him out and managed to have their photographs taken with him.

Our discussion of books leads me to ask how he works on his own books, several of which have been major best sellers. Normally he writes at home in his small study, but often times he must find a few spare hours in an airplane or hotel room. Some of the work on his current book, *Angels*, was completed at a friend's vacation home in Mexico, but even there a daily round of phone calls and correspondence took time from his writing chores. He enjoyed working on the angels book—he likes to dig into a subject, research it thoroughly, get to know and absorb all he can.

CHAPTER 6 TOWARD THE
ARENA

At five forty-five Grady is waiting in the driveway of the
Holiday Inn. "I just called upstairs," he says, "and Billy will
be down in a few minutes." As we stand and talk, a dark-
colored automobile pulls in back of Wilson's blue and white
Pontiac Grand Ville sedan. The car, which contains four
plain-clothes detectives, has been assigned as an escort and
will follow Grady into the stadium grounds.

I ask Grady what he thinks of the Crusade so far. He is
pleased with the response—the crowds have been large and
enthusiastic. "What you see here is a far cry from the old
days. I remember our very first Crusade. It was held in
Charlotte at the National Guard Armory. The meetings
lasted for three weeks, and the last night Gil Dodds, the
Olympic track star, ran around the indoor track, then
changed clothes and gave his testimony. This attracted two
thousand persons, and we thought we were really big stuff.
Then we went to Miami and started in a church, had to
move to a larger sanctuary and finally we ended up at the

Bayfront auditorium. From there it was the Lyric Theater in Baltimore, where a crowd of twenty-eight hundred came out the last night. Today we sometimes have twice that number come forward or sing in the choir."

Three men who grew together

I ask Grady if back in those early days he ever thought the ministry would develop and indeed mushroom as it has.

"No, we could never have imagined life would turn out this way," he replies. "You see, Billy and T.W. and I used to throw rocks at each other when we were boys. Billy was a very normal, regular guy. In fact, he was actually about the most shy and timid fellow in Charlotte. Now I see him preach before thousands of people, or hear him praised by a President or King, and no one could have ever predicted it would be like this. . . .

"Why, even his girl friend at Bible school in Florida dropped him because she wanted to marry someone who would be a successful minister."

I ask Grady how he accounts for Graham's incredible success. "The answer is the sovereignty of God asserting itself in this generation. We live in an age when frustration, uncertainty and the multitude of problems we face on a human level are driving people to seek spiritual answers. Billy Graham has been consistent as to the remedy for these problems."

As Grady is talking, Graham and T. W. Wilson approach the car and Billy jokes, "Jerry, you had better be careful with what Grady tells you."

We all laugh and step into the auto. I marvel at the easy rapport that exists between the three old friends. They have been through so many difficult and rewarding experiences, they have moved far beyond the constricted circles of Charlotte and the old-time South of their boyhoods, but they have not allowed fame and good fortune to diminish their mutual esteem and respect. I find a sense of satisfaction in the thought that these three men, all approaching the end of their middle years, can still appreciate one another and find it the most natural thing in the world to be in each other's company.

The relationship between Graham and the Wilsons, and to only a slightly lesser degree the evangelist's relationship to Cliff Barrows and George Beverly Shea, provides an insight into the stability of the Graham organization. The key people were there either at the beginning or even before the beginning, indeed years prior to the time when anyone in his wildest fancy could have expected that Billy Graham would be a world-famous religious leader.

Trailer headquarters

Billy is preoccupied with the *Mayaguez* incident. He recalls his late afternoon conversation with Harold Lindsell and he asks T.W. to ascertain the latest information on the affair. Grady takes some of the concern from Graham's face when he describes a meeting he had earlier with the mother of the pastor of Albuquerque's First Baptist Church. The woman told Wilson that her son, who was active in the Graham Crusade recently held in his city, was converted to Christ during the first Jackson Crusade in 1953.

"Yes," Billy says, "he's doing a fine job in Albuquerque and I'm delighted he came to Christ under my ministry."

Graham then asks T.W. if Johnny Cash has arrived and when the entertainer is due at the stadium. T.W. responds that Cash will visit with Billy at six forty-five in the evangelist's trailer. T.W. also mentions several other people who will see Billy for a few moments prior to the service.

When I visited the stadium I asked Charlie Riggs about the trailer, and he told me that Graham usually comes to the Crusade site about one hour before the service is scheduled to begin. He uses a trailer as a kind of field headquarters. Here he can greet important guests, take telephone calls and make last-minute preparations for the meeting. From a security standpoint, the trailer allows Graham to enter the meeting area long before the bulk of his audience gets to the stadium.

About ten minutes after our departure from the hotel,

Grady turns on to Woodrow Wilson Avenue, makes a right turn past the main parking lot and pulls up just in back of the end zone stands on the east side of the field. Billy quickly walks to the white and silver trailer, and Grady and T.W. join Sterling Huston and Don Bailey, who wait near the tunnel that leads under the stands. Each man carries a walkie-talkie and each wears a bronze button in his jacket lapel.

The walkie-talkies will facilitate internal communication and will enable the Team members to keep in contact with each other throughout the evening. The buttons signify that the wearer has access to the platform.

Don informs T.W. that a crew from Swedish television will film tonight's session but it will take them some time to set up, so they will not interview Graham in the trailer. However, they may want to shoot some footage of him in the vehicle.

I take a quick tour of the infield. A small army of technicians is setting up the TV lights and checking out camera locations. Other men are testing the sound system, and at the press table two of Cash's people are installing a control panel for the singer's special audio setup. On the platform itself, some workmen are erecting a canopy to protect the area around the lectern in case of rain.

This is Youth Night. In recent years every Crusade has featured one or two such nights, and quite generally young people make up about 40 per cent of the Crusade audiences. Graham is very concerned with reaching young people with his message, and he has been rather successful in holding their attention and winning their allegiance. T. W. Wilson sees Billy's rapport with youth as being built on "genuine frankness and compassion."

He adds, "These youngsters are seeking idols, whether they be sports stars, astronauts or rock musicians, and Billy is able to present the person of Christ as an attractive and viable alternative to the usual run of teen-age heroes."

Graham has visited many college and university campuses, and he has attended several rock festivals, protest gatherings and love-ins. In his book *The Jesus Generation*, published in 1971 during the height of student unrest, the evangelist described a confrontation with a "fiery-eyed, long-haired, radical, young post-graduate student." This young man pointed to the skyscrapers of Manhattan and in "a voice filled with hatred and bitterness said, 'We're going to burn it down and start all over again.'" To which Graham replied, "What are you going to rebuild in its place?"

Ethel Waters, Johnny Cash and June Carter

I walk over to the trailer and find Billy, who is immaculately dressed in a blue suit, white shirt and blue tie, talking to seventy-eight-year-old Ethel Waters, the venerable singer who has been a close friend of Graham since the first New York Crusade. The evening before, Miss Waters sang her famous, "His Eye Is on the Sparrow," and although the years have dimmed her vocal power her innate showmanship brought a standing ovation. She told the crowd, "In 1957, I, Ethel Waters, a three-hundred-and-eighty-pound decrepit old lady, rededicated my life to Jesus Christ, and boy, because he lives, just look at me now. I tell you because he lives; and because my precious child, Billy, gave me the opportunity to stand there I can thank God for the chance to tell you his eye is on all of us sparrows."

This evening Ethel looks radiant; she has about her a tremendous sense of personal dignity. The two friends discuss the progress of the Crusade, and Billy asks Miss Waters to join him in September at Lubbock.

"You know if I can, I'll be there. I so much enjoy being at a Crusade. Now I have to go up and join the choir rehearsal or Cliff will be wondering where I am."

Billy gets up from the couch and helps the singer to the door where two young women wait to escort Miss Waters to the choir section.

A minute or so later the door opens and Ken Chaffin comes in along with a medium-sized middle-aged man.

"Dr. Graham, I would like you to meet Rev. Harold Johnson. Rev. Johnson is attending the School of Evangelism. You may remember he wrote a note to you earlier in the week."

Billy puts out his hand and says, "Yes, of course, please sit down."

Johnson tells Graham how much the Crusade has meant to him, and Billy requests Johnson to lead in a word of prayer.

The minister asks for "a harvest of souls this evening," and when he has finished I notice a tear in the corner of his left eye.

"God bless you, brother," Billy says, and he takes Johnson's arm and accompanies him to the trailer door.

I later learn that Reverend Johnson had written to Graham describing his frustration with the ministry. He informed Graham he was about to leave his church and quite likely take a secular position. Last night he came out to the Crusade with a delegation from the School of Evangelism, and when the invitation was given he came forward to re-dedicate his life to Christ.

Graham goes to the refrigerator and takes a carafe of ice water from a shelf. His walkie-talkie crackles—it is Sterling Huston informing him that Johnny Cash and June Carter have just reached the stadium and will come directly to the trailer. Billy is very pleased. Johnny "is a wonderful man. Ruth and I have been in the Cash home and have felt the Christian atmosphere and the warmth John and June provide for their children. It's also been our joy to have them visit us in Montreat."

Johnny and Billy embrace, and June gives Graham a kiss on the cheek. Billy wants to know if the Cashes are being taken care of, are their rooms comfortable, have the arrangements for their performance been adequate. Cash assures Graham that everything is fine, and he tells Billy how happy he and June are to be in Jackson. "I'm only sorry we have to leave so soon, but this recording session has been planned for weeks now."

Billy understands, for he knows how complicated a person's schedule can get; he is very thankful that John and June could come at all.

I am intrigued by the scene in the trailer—here are three famous products of the South, and when they were growing up no one could have imagined that they would one day appear together before thousands of persons to witness to and preach their faith. It is true that Graham's middle-class background differs considerably from the poor origins of Johnny Cash, but at heart they are very similar. All the miles they have traversed and all the big towns they have visited and conquered have not changed them—they are very much at home in Jackson, a hospitable context for their activities. The Cashes and Graham know that the people who are now gathering in the Memorial Stadium understand them and are proud of them and their success. It is time for June and Johnny to join their accompanists, and Billy waves and says, "I'll see you on the platform."

Given in the name of the Lord

T.W. comes into the trailer. He has just been in touch with the local office of the National Weather Service and he gives Billy the forecast. "Radar shows heavy showers falling fifteen miles southwest of Jackson, and there should be a downpour in the stadium area in about one hour."

Billy asks T.W. to make sure his raincoat is handy and Wilson goes to the car to fetch it. Billy picks up a telephone and dials the Team office under the stands. He wants to know if anyone has seen Howard Jones—he would like the associate evangelist to come by for a moment.

Jones is located nearby and he quickly comes to the trailer. Billy wants to know how the meeting at the state penitentiary went and he is gladdened by Jones's report. Jones is an outstanding preacher. He has conducted several major Crusades in Africa—not long ago he held a pioneering series of meetings in Rhodesia and he has been invited back to that troubled nation for another round of services. In addition to his evangelistic responsibilities, Howard has been designated by Graham to direct the association's recently instituted Emergency Relief Fund.

Howard recalls that the fund came into being at the Twin Cities Crusade when Billy came up to him before one of the meetings and said, "Howard, I'm going to raise some real money tonight to feed the hungry in Africa." Graham then announced his intention to start the program, and when the offering was taken, seventy-one thousand dollars had been received.

Since that experience in Minneapolis, Graham has made appeals for the Emergency Fund after the budget of a Crusade has been raised. Unlike the humanitarian gestures extended by some evangelical organizations there are no strings attached to the Emergency Relief Fund grants. The money is channeled through existing reputable agencies—no hungry person has to listen to a sermon before receiving assistance. The rationale behind the program can be understood in the words printed on each fund check issued by the association, "Given in the name of the Lord Jesus Christ."

When one considers the long-standing evangelical reluctance to engage in social-action projects, the establishment of the Emergency Relief program was nothing short of courageous. It brings to mind the "third base" ministry articulated by E. V. Hill and is graphic proof of Graham's capacity to move beyond the narrow structures of twentieth-century American evangelicalism.

Actually the failure of Graham's predecessors and peers in the American evangelical movement to be involved with social reform represents an aberrant position. Nineteenth-century English evangelical leaders such as John Newton and William Wilberforce worked for the abolition of the slave trade as well as for industrial and prison reform, and a committed Scotch evangelical founded the British Labour Party. In America the outstanding revivalist George Whitefield collected funds for orphans, free blacks and immigrants during his open-air meetings, and Ohio's Oberlin College under the leadership of the great mid-nineteenth-century evangelist Charles Finney became a center of abolitionist activity.

Billy and Howard complete their talk, and Jones goes out to join his three daughters who perform as a singing trio at many Crusades. Billy radios Don Bailey and asks him if there is any further information available on the *Mayaguez* incident. I mention to Graham the conversation I had an hour or two earlier with Harold Lindsell, and the evangelist reiterates his view that world events are moving toward a flashing point.

"I really believe the coming of Christ may be much nearer than we think. I have a deep sense of urgency about my preaching; I want to reach so many people at this time of crisis."

Graham then mentions several world areas that are on the verge of exploding into open conflict. He is particularly concerned with conditions in the Middle East, as he has recently visited in the area and has held conferences with officials in Egypt and Israel. I joined him for the day and a half he spent in the Jewish state and for a moment we reminisce about some aspects of that visit.

Olympic flight 130 from Athens was five minutes early as it
landed flawlessly at David Ben Gurion International Airport
outside Tel Aviv. When Billy Graham and his associates
Grady Wilson and Walter Smyth stepped from the aircraft
they were met by their colleague Roy Gustafson, who has
led more than a hundred tours of Christian visitors to Israel.
Also waiting on the tarmac to meet the evangelist was
David Ben Dov, the director of the North American section
of the Israel Foreign Ministry. Billy looked tanned and fit,
but he was still feeling the aftereffects of a very serious case
of food poisoning suffered a few days earlier during a visit
to Cairo. In fact, his sudden and discomforting illness almost
caused Graham to cancel his Israel trip but the evangelist
was determined to make the journey. This, in combination
with a strict diet and loads of antibiotics, enabled Graham
to arrive in the Jewish state on schedule.

The sleek black limousine that was to transport Billy on

his whirlwind tour of Israel took him and his party to the
airport VIP lounge, where he rested while waiting for his
passport and other documents to be cleared. In the VIP
room Graham was interviewed by a reporter for Israel radio.
The evangelist indicated that this visit was occasioned by an
invitation from Prime Minister Itzhak Rabin and was his
first trip to Israel in several years.

With Golda Meir

From the airport Billy was driven to downtown Tel Aviv
for a meeting with an old friend, former Premier Golda
Meir. Mrs. Meir is now living quietly in retirement, working
on her papers and catching up with the activities of her two
young grandchildren. As Billy and the seventy-five-year-old
quintessential Jewish grandmother embraced, I was
reminded of a call I had from T. W. Wilson just after the
conclusion of the October 1973 Mideast war.

I was at a friend's house when T.W. reached me late on a
Thursday evening in early December to say that Billy, who
was then in St. Louis preparing for the start of a major Crusade in the Kiel auditorium, wanted Mrs. Meir, who was
meeting in Washington with President Nixon, to come to St.
Louis on Saturday night to address his Crusade audience.
T.W. stated that Graham realized this might be interpreted
as a political gesture, but he wanted the Prime Minister, the
people of Israel and his world-wide constituency to know
that he was solidly behind Israel in her continuing struggle
for survival.

Late that night, through the good efforts of Rabbi Marc
Tanenbaum of the American Jewish Committee, Mrs. Meir
was reached, but she had to refuse the invitation to come to
St. Louis because of a cabinet meeting scheduled for early
Sunday morning in Tel Aviv. Rabbi Tanenbaum told me
that when he reached Israeli Ambassador Simcha Dinitz at
his home, the envoy and Mrs. Meir were having a late sup-
per with Dr. Henry Kissinger, and Dinitz was careful not to
mention the Graham invitation until after the American

official had left for the evening. In any case, Graham was so eager to talk personally with the Premier that he had a special telephone line installed in his St. Louis hotel suite so that Mrs. Meir could talk to him confidentially. Graham asked me to go to Washington to give the number to Mrs. Meir, which I did, and on Friday, the day before she left for Israel, the two friends had a long and apparently useful telephone conversation. Graham later told me that he talked by phone with Mr. Nixon three times during the October War and in these conversations reminded Mr. Nixon that the overwhelming number of evangelical Christians in America were firm supporters of Israel.

The mutual esteem between Mrs. Meir and Graham was immediately apparent in their Tel Aviv session, and the former First Lady of Israel was delighted to autograph several copies of her recently published biography. Graham described his book on angels, and this occasioned an interesting conversation on the subject of these curious beings, with Mrs. Meir showing a keen knowledge of the biblical background related to the subject.

Walter Smyth and Grady had waited outside in the car while Billy talked privately with the former Premier. When Billy and Mrs. Meir finished their conversation, the two close associates of Graham were ushered into the apartment. Walter took a photograph of Mrs. Meir autographing a copy of her book for Ruth Graham. Later Billy had the photo pasted in the book under Mrs. Meir's inscription. This would be a special Christmas present for Ruth. A few days after the visit with the ex-Prime Minister, Billy remarked that Mrs. Meir's tome was, "about the greatest book I have ever read."

At 6 p.m. Billy and his associates were back in the Mercedes headed for Jerusalem. As the car eased through the late afternoon traffic Billy asked a number of questions about the development of Tel Aviv, a city that seems to add a new hotel or office building almost every day. For anyone interested in the history of the biblical period or in recent Middle East events the last half of the drive from Tel Aviv to Jerusalem has to rate as one of the most exciting in the world.

After passing through the Tel Aviv suburbs and the network of industrial parks, military camps and kibbutzim that make up the first part of the trip, one is suddenly thrust upon the wide expanse of the valley of Ajalon, the place where Joshua made the sun stand still. Here the view is breathtaking, and at sunset one is filled with the impression that he is in a very different and unique part of the world and that even greater thrills must be lurking behind the next curve or bend in the road.

Once past the valley the car enters the Bab el Wad, the narrow gorge that begins the ascent to Jerusalem. It was in this ravine that a great deal of the decisive fighting in Israel's War of Independence took place, and the sides of the road are still littered with burned out and destroyed vehicles, a conscious reminder of the difficulties and sacrifice that went into the creation of the Jewish nation. From the Bab el Wad the road continues to rise, and finally, after a series of hairpin turns, one looks up to see the lights of Jerusalem. Billy Graham was as excited as any ordinary tourist at seeing Jerusalem, and he remarked on how eager he was to discover what changes had been made since his last visit.

Soon the car turned on to Herzl Road and a few moments later Billy was inside the lobby of the Jerusalem Hilton Hotel. Graham and his party were greeted by the hotel's manager, Peter Demopolis, who truly had his hands if not his hotel filled that night. By a singular coincidence the Hilton housed three famous visitors to Israel: Billy Graham; UN Secretary General Kurt Waldheim, then on a swing through several regional capitals; and entertainer Frank Sinatra, in town for two benefit concerts. Security in the hotel and its immediate environs was very tight. Only two weeks before, a terrorist bomb blast in central Jerusalem had killed seven teen-agers (Billy would visit some of the injured from that blast the following day) and the authorities were taking no chances on having these world-renowned guests made uncomfortable.

In the old city of Jerusalem

At 8 A.M. the next morning Billy and his associates were driven to the office of Jerusalem's dynamic mayor, Teddy Kolleck. Kolleck had met Graham several times over the years and the two men greeted each other warmly. Kolleck was particularly interested in showing Graham the major restoration project being undertaken in the ancient Jewish quarter of the Old City of Jerusalem. After a chat, involving small talk and a discussion of local politics, Kolleck, his chief aide, Yissachar Ben Yaacov, and the Graham party headed in two cars for the Old City. The drive took Graham past the Avenue of the Paratroopers, the street that marked the pre-1967 border between Jordan and Israel. From there the mini-caravan drove due east, through the Jaffa Gate and then down the narrow lane that leads to the Jewish section of the Old City.

Kolleck directed the cars to a parking area next to a newly constructed Yeshiva for Jewish study, and the group walked downhill toward the Western Wall, the focal point of Jewish religious and national life. On the way to the wall the mayor pointed out the ruins of several ancient synagogues, and he also called attention to the series of archaeological excavations aimed at unearthing significant information about the Jewish past, particularly about the period from the return of the Jews from Babylon in 587 B.C. to the destruction of the Second Temple in A.D. 70.

Graham was especially interested in the findings concerning religious practice and he questioned Ben Yaacov about the controversial dig under way in the temple area. This excavation had been the subject of a bitter dispute between UNESCO and the Israeli government. The dig near the Temple Mount has also raised speculation that Israel plans to erect another temple in the same general area that housed the first two temples. Billy wanted to know if there was any truth to the rumors he had heard and read about in evangelical publications concerning the plans for another temple, and the mayor quickly put these conjectures to rest.

"We have absolutely no interest in constructing another temple," Kolleck said. "We feel the Western Wall itself is enough of a sacred place to provide a focus for Jewish spiritual observance. Also we are very concerned with the care of the religious shrines of other faiths, and this area we are now in has important meaning for Moslems."

Kolleck referred to the Temple Mount itself upon which the Dome of the Rock and the Al Aqsa Mosque are built. According to Islamic tradition the former contains the huge stone Abraham was to have used in the sacrifice of his son Isaac while the later shrine is built upon the spot from which the prophet Muhammed ascended into heaven. Kolleck made it clear that Israel has no intention of reconstructing the temple, although he indicated that he understood why there was a good deal of interest among evangelicals in such a project. Grady Wilson mentioned that some Christians feel the rebuilding of the temple would be connected with the return of Christ to earth, and Kolleck replied that he was familiar with this theory. Afterward the Graham party remarked on how impressed they were with the mayor's grasp of Christian history and with his understanding of evangelical views concerning Jerusalem and the Holy Land in general. As an observer somewhat familiar with both Jewish and Christian interests in Jerusalem, I was struck by the breadth of Kolleck's knowledge about the city he governs. In any case the Graham party was delighted to have the mayor show them the city he so obviously loves.

The next stop for Graham was the Western Wall itself. By this time it was a little after eleven and the broad plaza near the wall was beginning to fill up with tourists and the normal sprinkling of Israelis who come from all parts of the country to stand and watch the orthodox Jews pray and meditate in front of the wall. I could not of course read Graham's mind but he seemed both intensely interested and moved by the massive stone structure, the only remaining portion of the Second Temple.

Kolleck explained that when the Romans destroyed Jerusalem in A.D. 70 they left this wall, which in actuality formed the western part of the larger wall surrounding the outer courtyard of the temple grounds as a reminder to the Jews of the destruction of their nation. Kolleck then commented that the wall was a symbol of the survival of the Jewish people. As he made this remark, his voice, which is usually full of bounce and breeziness, became almost solemn. One could sense that for Teddy Kolleck no visit to the wall is ordinary or mundane. He seemed caught up in the remembrance of the tragic history of the Jewish people and what many see as the miraculous renewal and rejuvenation accomplished by the creation of the Jewish state. I also sensed that Graham and his associates were touched by Kolleck's demeanor, and the episode took on the character of one of those moments in which you can almost empathize with the inner spiritual experience of another human being.

As I listened to Kolleck at the wall and at other sites along the tour I couldn't help but think that other major cities would probably be in better condition if they had an enthusiast like Kolleck as their mayor.

From the wall the group walked through the "souk" or Arab market, which is a major center of interest for visitors to Jerusalem. I noted that even here, in an area six thousand miles from America and by no means a strong point of evangelical activity, Billy Graham was recognized and people clamored for his autograph. In fact the interest in Billy was so keen that even if he had wanted to he could not have stopped to buy a gift in one of the many stalls that line the narrow streets of the market.

Mount of Olives

After a fifteen-minute stroll the party walked through the Damascus Gate and the cars then circled the Old City and drove up the steep slope of the Mount of Olives. After passing through the busy Arab village on the hillside, the group arrived at the top of the mount, and stretched out beneath them was the Old City of Jerusalem, surely one of the world's most breathtaking sights. Teddy Kolleck explained that this view was most enchanting in the evening when one could see the lights of Jerusalem and its surrounding suburbs almost as far as Bethlehem, the town of Jesus' birth. He made a special point of calling attention to the Jewish cemetery located directly below the summit where a restoration project is repairing the many gravestones broken and destroyed during the period of Jordanian occupation from 1958 to 1967.

The Graham party was especially interested in the topography leading down to Gethsemane, where Jesus prayed during his last night on earth, and they asked about the route he took prior to his arrest. Kolleck gave a running account of the probable path Jesus traversed, and he then pointed to the areas inside the walls that were to play important roles in the events of his trial and crucifixion.

The panoramic view provided by the Mount of Olives gave the mayor the opportunity to discuss the seizure of the Old City during the June 1967 war. Kolleck called the group's attention to the Golden Gate, which is sealed and according to Jewish tradition not to be opened until the coming of the Messiah. This entrance provided the Israeli troops with the best route of access to the Old City and the Western Wall, but they would not blow open the gate in respect for the age-old Jewish beliefs about its Messianic significance. Instead, the paratroopers who liberated the Old City attacked through St. Stephen's Gate at considerable human cost.

Billy was very engrossed with this account, and as I observed him I thought back to a conversation I had had with Harold Lindsell concerning Graham's interest in Israel. Lindsell had asked if I was familiar with the film *His Land*, produced on location in Israel by World Wide Pictures in 1970.

This film, which was eventually viewed by over ten million persons in the United States and Canada, presented a thoroughgoing evangelical theological perspective on Israel while at the same time conveying a warm and sympathetic understanding of the reborn Jewish nation.

According to Lindsell, *His Land* illustrated Billy's deep concern for the people of Israel. There was an expression of interest that went far beyond the spiritual dimension and carried over into the political arena where Israel then and now is struggling for her life.

The night before Kolleck's tour I had asked Billy about how he was able to balance sympathy for Israel with concern for the status of Christians living in the Arab world. He has always been very careful to keep his contacts with these believers alive and on this visit to the Middle East he had spent two days in Cairo and met privately with a delegation of Christians from strife-torn Lebanon. Billy explained that he understands his ministry to be world-wide in scope and that he must never inhibit or shut out opportunities to minister particularly in situations where local Christians are troubled and seek out his presence and message.

The next stop on the itinerary was the residence of Israel's Prime Minister, Itzhak Rabin. Here Billy was graciously welcomed at the door by Leah Rabin. A few moments later, her husband came out of a small study and warmly greeted Billy and his associates. Rabin and Graham had met each other on several occasions when the ex-chief of staff of the Israel Defense Forces served as Israel's Ambassador to the United States. A few days before the Graham visit I had talked with Rabin, and I was impressed by both his grasp of the nuances of American religious life and his specific interest in the activities of evangelical Christians. Rabin told me that he had appeared before many church groups while serving in Washington and he had the impression that evangelicals made up the bulk of Israel's non-Jewish supporters in the United States.

For the Graham luncheon, the Prime Minister's office had invited a cross section of religious leaders and representatives of the foreign ministry and other government branches. One of the guests, Dr. M. Bernard Resnikoff, the representative in Israel of the prestigious American Jewish Committee, told Dr. Graham that his office was responsible for the distribution of *His Land* in Israel. Resnikoff also asked Billy to give regards to several World Wide Pictures executives with whom he had worked, including Frank

Jacobson, the talented producer of the film. Billy, Grady and Walter were especially happy to greet their old friend Bob Lindsay, a Southern Baptist official stationed in Israel, who lost a leg during the 1948 War of Independence. After lunch many of the guests asked Billy questions concerning biblical prophecy and the role of Israel in Christian eschatology.

The Jewish participants were interested in learning Graham's views on the future of Israel, and Billy replied that he believed the establishment of Israel was a forerunning event connected with the return of Christ to the earth. Billy went on to explain his interpretation of the biblical position on the Second Coming of Christ, and a lively theological discussion ensued. One of the rabbis, upon learning that Billy was working on a book about angels, remarked that his library contained a volume on the subject but that it was quite old and did not reflect the kinds of ideas Graham would likely express.

When the luncheon ended, Billy and the Prime Minister went into another room for a private conversation. As they came out Billy remarked, "You know, when you visited me in my Washington hotel room a few years ago I didn't realize that one day you would be Prime Minister Rabin." Rabin, who is not generally known for levity, smiled and replied, "Neither did I."

Visiting the wounded

The last stop on Graham's day in Jerusalem was at the Hadassah Hospital. Billy's basic purpose in coming to the huge ultramodern facility was to visit the victims of two recent terrorist attacks, one involving a bomb planted in downtown Jerusalem, the other a night raid on a settlement in the Golan Heights bordering Syria. Billy went directly to the wards where the injured were housed, and it was apparent that several of these unfortunate people were in desperate condition.

One man had been blinded by the bomb and was not expected to live. Billy, who has spent many hours visiting

American troops wounded in both the Korean and Vietnam wars, patiently talked with a number of the injured. A man who miraculously survived the force of the bombing showed Billy a few pieces of shrapnel that were taken from his head. Another patient, his entire body covered with bandages, shook Graham's hand and thanked him for coming.

After the ward tour Grady and Walter went to the hospital cafeteria for a cup of coffee while Billy, who was still feeling the aftereffects of his food poisoning episode, was examined by two house physicians. Before the group left the hospital grounds they were taken to the chapel that houses the famous Chagall windows depicting the twelve tribes of Israel, and Yissachar Ben Yaacov, Teddy Kolleck's aide, pointed to the window that represents the tribe for which he is named. The group was much impressed by the beauty and intricate design of each frame, and Billy, who soaks up information on new and challenging subjects, very rapidly asked a number of questions concerning the composition of the materials used by Chagall. Several days later in Paris he came across a magazine article describing the artist, and this was immediately put into his file for later reading.

While the official portion of his day ended with the hospital visit, Billy still had important work to do. Back in his room at the hotel Billy worked over the text for the "Hour of Decision" broadcast and then he recorded the message with the assistance of a technician sent over from the Israel Television Service. When the recording session was completed, Grady took a taxi to the Television Service headquarters, where two copies of the tape were made. One tape would be airmailed to the Walter Bennett advertising agency in Chicago, and the other copy would be forwarded directly to Cliff Barrows in Greenville, South Carolina. In an emergency, Cliff could dip into his well-stocked library of Billy's Crusade messages to provide a substitute sermon. Billy, however, likes to keep the "Hour of Decision" as current as possible and he prefers fresh material. Thus the message that was taped in the Jerusalem hotel suite was heard around the world less than three weeks later.

An army of Crusade volunteers

While Graham has been in the trailer, a small army of Crusade volunteers has reported to the stadium. Ushers meet with their captains in front of the west stands, choir members climb onto the benches behind the platform, counselors assemble under the north bleachers. At the counselor gathering station, supervisors form the counselors in sections of fifteen with seven men, six women and two young adults in each group.

Fifteen hundred counselors will be deployed this evening in thirty-nine separate areas. When the invitation is given and people begin to leave their seats to walk to the stadium infield, the supervisors will match up counselors and inquirers, and if all goes according to the carefully prepared instructions each inquirer will find a counselor at his side when he joins the crowd in front of the platform.

The counselor program at Jackson is headed up by David Bradford, a thirty-five-year-old CPA and member of the Crusade steering committee. He was first contacted by a friend who knew that Bradford, who is a former naval officer, had been active with the Navigators while in service and that he was a regular listener to the "Hour of Decision" radio broadcast. Five months before the Crusade began, David and eleven other men met for Bible study. When the three-week course was completed Bradford and the others started their own classes, and their students in turn organized further classes, thus widening the circle of potential counselors and Crusade workers.

As a member of the steering committee Bradford has met Graham, and he is very impressed by the evangelist and his grasp of the world situation. "He speaks with real knowledge and insight, he certainly fulfilled my expectations."

This evening Bradford will need a strong complement of teen-age and young adult counselors, and he has spent part of the day in the Crusade office going over his lists and making phone calls to a number of volunteers.

Crowds are coming

It is seven-fifteen and long lines are forming at the stadium entrances. Buses pull into the parking lot at the rate of six a minute and out on Interstate 55, a stalled car blocks the lane leading to the stadium exit. Outside the south gates five pickets solemnly distribute leaflets claiming that "Billy Graham is a captive of modernism."

For the most part, however, the incoming crowd is good humored, there are jokes about the impending rain, "it's real Baptist weather tonight," people courteously allow others to scamper ahead of them up the concrete steps to the wooden grandstands.

Overhead a police helicopter scans the scene and a passing freight train sends a long whistle of greeting to the rapidly assembling throng.

John Innes at the organ, and Tedd Smith, the long-time Graham pianist, warm up their instruments, ushers hand out a combination program/song sheet, "Tonight Is Youth Night, the Special Musical Guests Tonight Are Johnny Cash and June Carter."

The one-page paper also advertises a biography of Billy Graham, at $1.50, and contains a coupon good for a year's free subscription to *Decision* magazine.

At seven-sixteen Graham, accompanied by Grady and T. W. Wilson, leaves the trailer and walks about twenty-five feet into the tunnel under the north stands. He quickly passes an office, a small storeroom and enters the dressing room that has been adapted into a staging point for the platform guests.

Although everything he has done in the last twelve hours has been only a prelude to what awaits him on the field, the evangelist appears quite relaxed as he stops to chat with each of the men and women in the room. His smile is as easily extended as his large right hand and he puts the platform participants at ease. As he completes his circuit of the cramped space he raises his voice in a brief prayer. "God bless all of you for coming. We are going to have some rain but the Lord is in control and we will give him the glory and the honor."

Just as he is about to re-enter the tunnel he encounters an elderly, distinguished-looking man. They embrace. Twenty-three years before, the gentleman was a driving force behind the first Jackson Crusade. The old man is touched that Graham remembers him, he stammers a greeting, Billy takes his arm and asks him to accompany him and join the others on the platform.

Sterling Huston, who is directly behind Graham, presses the button on his walkie-talkie and asks that another chair be placed on the platform. Graham leaves the tunnel and enters the infield. He is quickly spotted, and a wave of excitement moves through the stadium. A hundred voices as in unison utter, "There he is, that's Billy Graham."

Billy reaches the platform and takes an aisle seat in the second row. The crowd is still filing in as Cliff Barrows, dressed in a bright yellow sports jacket, moves to the lectern and begins the service.

The choir is into the second verse of the stirring hymn, "Great Is Thy Faithfulness" when I cross the infield and move in the direction of the press section. I sit between Harold Lindsell and the sound engineer who will operate Johnny Cash's highly sophisticated audio equipment.

I study Lindsell and find him as serious and intent as the other Graham associates and Team members I will observe during the evening. Most of these men have sat in stadiums like this throughout the world. Over the years they have been part of a hundred Crusades, they have attended thousands of services and all would be justified in being somewhat blasé if not jaded. But I see no signs of ennui or battle fatigue. Lindsell is taking notes, Ken Chaffin and Bob Ferm, a former professor at Houghton College, will carefully listen to Graham. They know the evangelist is a perfectionist and he is always interested in a critique on the form, style or content of his delivery, although it is difficult to imagine how the technique of this man who has spoken before more people than any other person in recorded history could possibly be more effective.

George Beverly Shea

Mrs. Florence Greentree, the attractive and charming Crusade prayer chairman, gives a greeting and presents the pastor of a large downtown church who asks God to "bless your servant, Billy Graham, and hold off the rain if it be in accordance with your divine will." Cliff springs from his seat and introduces "America's beloved gospel singer, George Beverly Shea."

The soloist is dressed in a brown checked suit and matching tie. He has been with Graham since the early months of 1944 when he joined the then Western Springs, Illinois, pastor on the Sunday evening radio show "Songs in the Night." Shea was then a station manager and had already achieved a measure of success as a performer on the ABC radio network program, "Club Time."

Tonight Shea sings one of his most famous compositions, "I'd Rather Have Jesus." The bass baritone's voice, so familiar to "Hour of Decision" listeners, has lost some of its strength and clarity, but there is still a haunting quality to Shea's presentation and he finishes to warm applause.

Barrows is on his feet telling the crowd that tomorrow will be Athlete's Night with testimonies from Ken Hutcherson of the Dallas Cowboys and the Kansas City Chiefs' Andy Hamilton. In addition, a special "Teammates for Christ" rally will be held just before the Crusade service at a nearby high school field. Cliff runs down the list of participants and, a lifelong baseball fan, I smile when I hear him include Dave "Boo" Ferris, former Boston Red Sox pitching ace. Barrows then asked those in the crowd who attended the previous evening's meeting to wave their programs, and about one third of the audience responds.

As the choir begins the popular hymn "Blessed Assurance," Governor Waller and his family leave their limousine and walk toward the running track. Charlie Riggs races over to greet the Wallers and he asks the governor to sit on the platform. Waller declines—he would rather join his family, who usually sit on folding chairs in front of the east end zone.

In the stands just above the state's first family a woman repeats the words of the hymn in sign language to a group of mute persons, while on the hillside between the end zone and the south grandstand, several teen-agers lounge and smoke, seemingly oblivious to the crowd and activity that surround them. A dozen or so uniformed policemen sit on the running track. They are available for crowd control, but thus far their services are not needed. The Tennessee delegation sits on camp chairs directly opposite the platform. These seats are reserved for their use each evening and next to them are seated forty-six Choctaw Indians, who have come from the Old Canaan Baptist Church, eighty-one miles away.

A local pastor is well into a prayer seeking "great blessings and renewal for the citizens of Mississippi," when someone in the crowd becomes seriously ill. Within minutes a team of white-coated medical aides carries the stricken person down a ramp and into an ambulance which is positioned at the west end of the stadium.

Cliff introduces Billy Graham, who will bring words of greeting and then present the evening's special guests, Johnny Cash and June Carter. Graham asks the audience to observe a minute of silent prayer for the person who has just become ill. He then mentions a "great black leader, a man originally from Mississippi, now pastor in a northern state who came to visit me yesterday and who told me, 'You know I would rather live in Mississippi than any state in the North,' and I think that says something for Mississippi." I notice that in his desire to establish rapport with the audience, Graham makes many local allusions. He speaks of "going down to Biloxi," he states, "The people of Mississippi are generous, warm and friendly," he says, "we are in the stadium in which Ole Miss plays." Later Cliff will correct Billy and tell him that Mississippi State University also uses the Memorial Stadium and the crowd will enthusiastically applaud.

Graham becomes very serious and mentions the attack on

the American merchant ship *Mayaguez*. The vessel has been fired upon and seized in the Gulf of Siam about sixty miles from the Cambodian coast. The crew has been captured, and Graham asks, "What will the American response be? These things are happening all over the world," he continues, "and the scriptures say there will come a day when the weak will say, 'I'm strong,' those little nations will twist our tail and kick us and beat us, and there is nothing we can do about it; and we've already reached that stage. I'm glad I'm not President—I tell you something would be done about it." This last remark elicits strong applause. The evangelist announces the offering is about to be received, and as he speaks, a rain shower spreads over the open stadium. People reach for umbrellas, and on the platform Grady Wilson places Graham's tan raincoat on the evangelist's seat.

Before the offering

Before the offering is taken, Graham indicates that the funds will go to his organization's Emergency Relief Fund, and he explains something of the purpose of the relief program.

"Did you know that the world right now probably is on the verge of the greatest famine in the history of mankind? Right now at this moment, ten thousand people a day are starving for lack of food. In some parts of Africa, I read the other day, they have eaten everything they can lay their hands on, cats, dogs, mice, birds, bark off the trees, manure and in some cases even each other, just to stay alive. We in America are 6 per cent of the world's population, but we consume 50 per cent of the world's goods. A food conference in Rome was told there's only one problem in the world today—not two problems, not three, just one—the question of feeding the world's huge population. One third of the world is well fed, one third of the world is starving. The Rome conference said the human race stands at the greatest crisis of its existence, and it's very doubtful that we can survive as a human race. And Jesus said that you and I as

Christians have a responsibility. I was hungry and you gave me food, and I was thirsty and you gave me drink. Have you been doing that? Our association, which is called the Billy Graham Evangelistic Association, has set up an emergency relief fund, and if you want to send money to us and earmark it for that, we'll see that it gets to the people. We will guarantee that 90 per cent of it gets there. Ten per cent has to be kept out by different agencies and so forth for the transportation and all the rest of it, but when we write a check to someplace in Africa or some agency, we put on that check, given in the name of the Lord Jesus Christ. We believe that we have a responsibility to those who are hungry and especially to those fellow believers in other parts of the world who are suffering." Ushers circulate through the stands passing out cardboard pails that resemble the containers used by fast food chicken franchises. Almost everyone seems to participate, with paper currency rather than small change making up the bulk of the contributions.

Man in Black

The evangelist then calls on Johnny Cash. "Tonight I do not need to introduce our special guest because he's known all over America and all over the world, all you have to do is talk about the man in black and he's talking about it in a brand new book that he's written, a spiritual autobiography that I know is going to be a best seller. My wife and I are planning to buy copies and give them away as Christmas presents this year, because we believe in this couple. Tonight, I'm proud and honored and thrilled and flattered to present my very good and warm friend in Christ, Johnny Cash."

As Cash and his troupe come to the front of the platform the red light of the television camera is activated. The televised portion of the evening's program will include Cash, another hymn, a selection from Bev Shea, Billy Graham's sermon and the invitation with a closing hymn. This schedule fits into the Crusade pattern long ago established by the

Graham organization. The formula is highly successful, and when I ask a Team member why there has been little innovation over the years in the Crusade program, he responds that "like everyone else Graham falls into a certain pattern—he has discovered what works for him and there is really little need for change."

Cash and June Carter come to the podium. The Cashes have journeyed to Jackson to sing, but they also wish to speak to the Crusade audience.

"Thank you, Billy, for all those kind words. June and I appreciate them very much. *Man in Black*, as he said, is an autobiography, a spiritual autobiography. I told him just before the service tonight that I'm glad to say that the spiritual autobiography is very incomplete, because we have a lot that we're trying to learn and a lot that we are still trying to do. It was almost eight years ago that we renewed our total commitment to Jesus Christ, and I just wanted to say in case anybody had any doubt that I'm a Christian and I'm awfully proud to say so." The Cash company sings one of Johnny's recent compositions, "The Ragged Old Flag"—and Johnny introduces June Carter.

"Ladies and gentlemen, here is my right arm, the woman in my life and the sweetest thing I've ever known, my wife, June Carter." June turns to Johnny and says, "That's the most wonderful belated Mother's Day present that a woman could hear. Bless your heart. I would like to say praise the Lord for that ragged old flag and for that ragged old husband of mine. You know we have so much to be thankful for and I stop daily to count my blessings, but tonight I was thinking as he sang 'The Ragged Old Flag' how much we truly must have to be thankful for in these United States of America. To have the ragged old flag hanging there is fine, and the greatest blessing is that you can have Jesus Christ in your heart because that's where he lives within me, in my heart. And I'm proud to say as a mother and a wife in the heart of my family as well. Billy, thank you for inviting us—we're so glad to be with you, so glad to be a part of this great Crusade here in Jackson, Mississippi."

The Message

When the song is finished John and June return to their seats while the rest of their group of musicians leave the platform and find seats along the running track. The rain is falling in steady, slanting sheets, and the canopy protecting the podium area is rapidly filling with water. Bev Shea, attired in a plastic slicker, sings the great Crusade favorite "How Great Thou Art," and then Billy Graham, wearing his raincoat and partially protected by the canopy and an umbrella held by a committee member, begins his message. For his text he has chosen Mark 10:17–22, one of the New Testament's most familiar passages, the story of the rich young man who came to Jesus seeking eternal life.

"Now there are many things I would like to say about this passage tonight. It's the story of a young aristocrat coming to Jesus Christ. Handsome, we can suppose, certainly wealthy and young, but he was like thousands of young people and older people alike here tonight. He was seeking something else in life. He wasn't satisfied with the way life was at the moment. The pressures of life were too great. He might have been a university student, he might have been a senior student, I don't know. But right now we have a phenomenon that's been sweeping America for about eight or ten years. Younger people have suddenly become interested in religion, once again. For a while it was the middle-aged. It was my generation that seemed to be interested. Now my generation became more materialistic and secularistic and it has been young people coming along that have talked of spiritual things and talked about God. Some of them are looking in the wrong place. Some of them are looking in the Eastern religions, some of them are looking in the occult, but thousands of them have been turning to Jesus Christ. Now as I look on young people today I want to give you eleven things that I see among young people, and I'm old enough to say 'you young people.' I'm fifty-six years of age if you want to know my age. I have five children and nine grandchildren and two on the way. So tonight I want you to see yourselves the way I see you.

"Firstly, I believe there is a breakdown of home life, and it has led to moral and spiritual void. Even in some of the finest Christian homes, the God has become television. That little set we gather around—the only time the family is quiet, the only time the family has any little reverence is around that set. It used to be around the family Bible, it used to be around God, it used to be around prayer but now about the only time you can get the family together is if they agree on a certain program, and if they don't, most homes now have two sets so you divide the family. But there is a spiritual void, and when you think of one out of every two or three marriages breaking up, you have millions of young people being thrown out without the roots of a father and mother at home; and then in the homes that stay together, you have a lack of love between parents many times, and the young people feel this and they are affected psychologically and spiritually.

"Secondly, I find a tremendous dissatisfaction among young people with their lives as they are. A young person told me just the other day, 'I don't know what's wrong. I've got everything. I am a senior at the university but,' he said, 'I'm just dissatisfied with myself.' I said, 'Do you know why?' I said, 'Everybody has this same type of dissatisfaction until they find it in Jesus Christ.'

"And then, thirdly, I find in this generation of young people that sexual relationships don't provide the emotional closeness they thought they would. They are not finding the peace and happiness and the kicks and the deep satisfaction they thought they would find in all the so-called sex freedom. It has brought about a whole new set of psychological problems that affect them the rest of their lives, especially their future marriage.

"And then, fourthly, I find tremendous loneliness among young people. They can have friends, they can be in a crowd but there is also loneliness. You know why. You're lonely for God. You were made for God. You were made in God's image and you are lonely for him and don't know it.

We had one of the great psychiatrists of the country here the other night, and he said to me, when he came into the little trailer, that one of the great problems he has to deal with in his great psychiatric clinic is the problem of loneliness on the part of young people. Jesus can be closer than a brother. He can settle that loneliness. You see, you were made for God, for fellowship with God, and without God there is loneliness. Give your life to Christ tonight and never know another lonely moment.

"Then, fifthly, I find among people, young people, restlessness. They're very restless. Now a certain amount of restlessness during a teen-age period is normal. I've had five teen-age children and they were all restless. From a parent's point of view, they just had more energy than we had—that was really the problem. Sixthly, there's another kind of deeper restlessness that I'm talking about. I'm not talking about just getting up and running around and jumping around and riding a motorcycle and all those things. That comes with being a teen-ager. But there is a restlessness where they don't find peace and rest until they come to know Christ in a personal way.

"Then, seventhly, there is a feeling of emptiness and purposelessness. They haven't found purpose and meaning in their lives, so they are empty and they are bored. Let Christ come into your heart and fill that emptiness and take that boredom away.

"And then, eighthly, I find that many young people are despondent. They despair easily. They get discouraged, they get down in the dumps, they have depressions, and many of them are going to see psychiatrists and psychologists and clergy, trying to get something to pick them up, and a great many prescriptions today are being given to young people that need a little pickup.

"And then, ninthly, I find that for this generation of young people it's almost impossible for them to make decisions. About vocation, marriage, moral values, if there is a moral code or a moral absolute to make a decision about it.

"And then, tenthly, I find a sense of guilt, and they don't know why. But it's there and it causes all kinds of psychological problems. Well, of course, we are guilty. We have broken God's law. There is a right kind of guilt. There is a psychological guilt that's wrong, but there's a right kind of guilt in which you are guilty before God of breaking God's law, and that's called sin and it needs to be repented of, and it needs to be brought to the cross, and then don't let the devil put that guilt back on you. When you are forgiven by God, you are forgiven, and God not only forgives, he forgets, and when you are justified in the sight of God that means just as though you have never sinned.

"Come to Christ tonight. Let him take that guilt away. Then, eleventhly, I find that disillusionment is beginning to grow, and I'm delighted at this, and I hope I'm right. I read it in one of the magazines—our disillusionment with drugs as the answer to the problems that young people were using five or six or seven or eight years ago, when they thought that LSD and all the rest of it were the ultimate of experience, and now they are beginning to be educated to the fact that this is destructive.

"Now when you come to Jesus Christ I want to tell you something; in one way there is a high but that's very dangerous, because when you come to Christ it is not always living on a high. There are periods when you will get discouraged, just like other people, but that doesn't mean that you have lost Christ. There are two men in the Old Testament, two of the greatest men, that said 'God kill me.' Moses said, 'These people are too much for me, Lord, just kill me now'—and Elijah said, 'Lord, slay me, Jezebel is after me.' And you know the Lord came and ministered to both of them. God understands when you get discouraged. You see we're giving a false teaching if we teach that you come to Christ and you're always on top. Life isn't that way. Read the Psalmist. But let me tell you, your highs become more and more permanent and the highs are much longer lasting and much deeper and much greater, and after you have learned the ways of God and you've learned to walk with the Lord, it becomes a wonderful, thrilling life. Problems? Yes. Persecution? Yes. Misunderstanding? Yes. That all goes with taking your stand for Christ and it's all part of discipline.

"Now what about you? I think that many of you are like this young man. You've been searching for something. This young man might not have known exactly what he was searching for. He said, Lord, I want eternal life. In eternal life he meant I want to have a successful life here and now. I don't mean material prosperity, he already had that. I mean a successful inner life. The second thing he meant, I want eternal life in the sense of the future. I want to know that when I die I'm going to heaven."

They listen with rapt attention

Graham is thirty minutes into his message but the audience remains very quiet. There is hardly any movement in the stadium—even the pouring rain does not appear to bother the crowd as they listen with rapt attention to the evangelist. The sermon is relatively simple, there is nothing intellectually challenging or even stimulating. As Graham talks, a person who had never heard of him would not perceive that he is listening to a world-famous personality. The message does not reveal that Graham has enjoyed personal contact with important or extraordinary persons, nor do his comments suggest any unusual learning or life experiences. His remarks exhibit little consistency—there appears to be an outline, but he jumps from one point to another without a clear or easily recognizable transition. He does quote quite liberally from the scripture; several times his left arm shoots up, the large black Bible he favors in the pulpit clearly visible in his outstretched hand. Indeed the one integrating factor in the message is his employment of biblical language and imagery.

I recall Harold Lindsell's analysis of Graham's preaching. "He falls into line generally with the great evangelists of the ages. If you read the sermons of Charles Haddon Spurgeon you will not find contemporaneity. Jonathan Edwards would speak only in contemporary terms about his congregants' sin. Moody always preached in a biblical context, as did

Charles E. Fuller. Billy has been more interested in contemporary events, but his preaching is based on two convictions. First, the word of God has power and will not return void and, second, the Holy Spirit prepares the listener for an encounter with Christ through the word."

Despite the rain, Graham gamely continues. "He came with urgency, he ran to Jesus. There was an urgency about it, and there is an urgency about you. I'll tell you why. We don't know what day tomorrow is going to be. The Bible says remember the Creator in the days of our youth, but there is a different urgency in our generation. Our America, this country, and the world are changing more rapidly than at any time in the history of the whole human race since the days of Noah, and it changed rapidly in those days. In forty days and forty nights it was wiped out. We've got the ability right now to wipe ourselves out for the first time since the flood. There are many nations working on the atomic bomb —you are going to see things that are going to tear the human race apart. You're going to have to live through it or die in it. I hope that isn't true, but I think it's going to be true. The Bible teaches that anti-Christ or the spirit of anti-Christ is everywhere. There's an urgency about coming to Christ. Come to Christ while you can. There's an urgency because of this Crusade. Thousands of people have prayed— did you know that I was asked by a newpaper reporter tonight when I thought we'd be back to Jackson for another Crusade. I said, 'Well, the next time I'll probably have to be rolled up in a wheelchair.' When will we ever see a crowd like this, in a stadium like this again in Jackson? Maybe never. Thousands have prayed and thousands have worked and thousands have given, and God has prepared your heart and God has spoken to you, and you know that you have to make a commitment to Christ. The Bible says my spirit shall not always strive for man. Unless God, the Holy Spirit, makes you uncomfortable and brings you and draws you, you can't come to Christ. And he's doing that tonight in this meeting; and then, thirdly, he had the right attitude of humility, he didn't come up to Christ with his shoulders back and say,

'Look what a great guy I am.' He fell down before Christ and said, 'Lord, I know there's something wrong with my life. I need something else. I want eternal life.' That was an amazing sight, this rich young aristocrat falling at the feet of the penniless prophet of Nazareth, who was on his way to being an outlaw and was going to be crucified in a short time as a common criminal. But this young man didn't care who saw, he came in the open, publicly, to Christ, and he asked the right question. What did he ask? He said, 'what must I do?'

"*Psychology Today*, a magazine for psychologists, polled their readership recently and asked what they wanted more than anything in the world. We had a girl last night who sang. Most of you didn't know who she was. But she's been written up in some magazines and papers, and it's been speculated that she's the richest woman in the world, since the death of her father. I don't know whether that's true or not. I've never discussed money with her. She was here because she is a dynamic Christian. She was here because she has a beautiful voice, and she's dedicated to Christ. What would you rather have more than anything in the whole world? 'Oh, boy, if I could just get my hands on a million bucks.' 'Or if I could get that girl to say yes that I've been chasing.'

"No, eternal life. In the survey that *Psychology Today* made, they said the thing they wanted more than anything in the world is eternal life. If you have eternal life, you have everything. You know that little ad on television—if you have your health, you have just about everything? Well, I want to tell you if you don't have spiritual health and if you don't have Christ you haven't got anything, because this body is going to die. This brain is going to stop someday, this heart is going to stop someday.

"We need eternal life, and eternal life is provided by the Lord, Jesus Christ. He can give you eternal life tonight, now. You don't have to wait till you die to get eternal life, you can get it right now. I want you to get out of your seat and come right now and receive Christ."

Coming forward in the rain

I am surprised by the rapid transition to the invitation. As he articulates these words there is a definite expectancy in the crowd. The overwhelming number of people present are familiar with the pattern of a Crusade session, they know that Graham will conclude his sermon with the invitation, they are prepared to hear him make the offer of salvation through personal commitment to Christ and some begin to leave their seats when he says, "I want you to get out of your seat . . ." Soon, within a few minutes, a remarkable number of people are coming toward the platform from every section of the stadium.

The rain, already heavy and chilling, increases in intensity —it is now a good old-fashioned downpour—but those who do not come forward remain in their seats. This is a moment of high drama and the audience seems to find a vicarious pleasure in watching the hundreds of people fill up the space beside the platform.

Just after the invitation is given, an announcement is made, "Will doctor 299 go to St. Dominics for an emergency?" Then as the inquirers and counselors gather, Graham speaks to the growing assemblage. He asks them to pray with him and he describes the packet of materials that the counselors will leave with the inquirers.

After eight minutes he turns in the direction of the TV camera and gives a special invitation to the viewing audience. "Hundreds of people are coming forward tonight in Jackson, Mississippi. Won't you come to Christ now? There may never be a better opportunity than now to give your life to Christ."

Graham then looks out at the stands and asks others to come forward.

"God may be working on your heart," he says. "The Bible says, 'Now is the day of salvation, this is the accepted time.' I want you to leave your seats and come down here in front of the platform and join these people who have decided to make Jesus Christ their personal Lord and Savior. Your friends will wait for you. If you've come by bus, the bus will wait. I want you to come and accept Christ as Lord."

Unlike other evangelists Graham does not plead, cajole or beg. The invitation is low-key. There is little doubt that Graham is earnest, and as you look at Grady Wilson studying the faces of the crowd from the back of the platform and the other members of the Team who are circulating around the infield you realize that this is very crucial indeed, all the telephone calls, letters, meetings, breakfasts, appointments, offerings, airplane rides, miles of travel and weeks away from family and everyday preoccupations come down to the wrestling for souls that is going on in front of the platform.

Here in a thirty-yard square, counselors and inquirers are grappling with issues of greater significance than the *Mayaguez*, or integration or the anticipated price of cotton.

For most of the people who have come down from the stands at Graham's invitation, this is a moment of truth. They are undergoing a crisis experience that will shape their thought processes, personal habits and perhaps their destinies into the indefinite future.

Whether it is God, or Billy Graham or a childhood memory brought to the surface by a prayer, or the sense of community produced by sitting in an arena with thousands of other people, something has moved the inquirers from their seats and has placed them in an existential situation where they are ready to admit inadequacy, sinfulness and need. As I walk among these individuals I nod my head in agreement with the words Sherwood Wirt uttered as I left the hotel to come out to the stadium, "There is nothing going on in the world like what you will see out there tonight."

In the infield a woman counselor looks up at a middle-aged peer from her wheelchair; a young white woman talks with a black teen-ager and promises to call her the next morning; a heavy-set black pastor works with a well-dressed, thirtyish white man; two marines in dress whites are counseled by an air force corporal; a group of five elderly VA hospital patients wearing bathrobes and pajamas listens somberly to a counselor; Judy Butler, Charlie Riggs's secretary, leads a young girl from the county reformatory to Christ.

Later with the assistance of Roger Palm of *Decision* magazine, I will learn of a three-year-old girl who asked her parents to take her forward; a church deacon who told his counselor, "The hardest thing for me is that I am going to have to tell my pastor and fellow deacons that I've been living a hypocritical life all these years"; the husband and wife who were caught in the I-55 traffic jam while on the way to a doctor's office so came to the rally, and who went forward together; the fifteen-year-old boy who walked on crutches from the top tier of the stadium; the manufacturing executive who removed a gold Playboy Club card from his wallet saying, "I won't be needing this any more"; the young man with a speech problem who went forward and discovered his counselor was a speech therapist.

Drama in the infield

One does not have to be a believer to sense the drama of what is happening on the infield. I truly hope that those who have come forward will experience positive and long-lasting changes in their lives, that they will have a more solid foundation than before upon which to cope with the complexities, difficulties and disappointments of life, but I am also interested in the racial composition of the inquirers and struck by the large number of blacks, and particularly black teen-agers, who have responded to Graham's invitation. Jim Pearson, a local pastor and counselor supervisor looks across the infield and says, "The number of blacks coming forward is very encouraging to those of us who want to see things in Mississippi on an equal footing between the races, in the sight of man as well as in the sight of God."

The quest that is involved in the inquirers' decision to come forward in response to Graham's invitation is of keen interest—I wish I could talk to all of the people who stand in front of the platform. This, of course, is impossible, but I do nevertheless manage to speak to what I take to be a representative sampling of inquirers.

Brother and sister

Thirteen-year-old Jimmy Wheatly came to the Crusade with his sister, Sue. Jimmy has attended church and Sunday school for as long as he can remember. He is an officer in the Training Union of his Baptist church, but until tonight he has never made a confession of Christ.

Sue Wheatly, who is two years older than her brother, accepted Christ at a summer camp last year. Jimmy and Sue were seated high in the grandstand, and when the invitation was given, Sue prayed very earnestly for her brother to respond. At first Jimmy stayed put; he seemed distracted and Sue worried that he would not go forward. Then as the choir continued singing the revival hymn, "Just as I Am," she turned to Jimmy and asked him if he wanted to come to Christ. Jimmy said yes, and he wondered if it would be all right for Sue to accompany him to the infield. Sue was more than happy to comply, and the two young people walked down the concrete stairway arm in arm.

They were not talking, but . . .

Tom and Ellen Bryant came to the Crusade as a favor to the Cushings, their next-door neighbors. Laura Cushing has been active in the prayer campaign, and Ellen attended one of the prayer sessions in Laura's home.

The Bryants, who are both in their late twenties, are not church members and have been in Jackson only a few months. Tom and Ellen have been having marital difficulties —Ellen did not want Tom to leave his job in northern Virginia to take the position with the Jackson bank. She grew up in the Washington suburbs, and almost all of her family and close friends live in or near the nation's capital. Ellen has few friends in Jackson and she feels very lonely and depressed.

When they arrived at the meeting tonight, the Bryants were barely communicating. Tom had had a busy and tiring day, and, to make matters worse, Ellen had arranged for them to travel with the Cushings so they would not be able to leave the stadium until Larry Cushing finished his counseling duties. The heavy downpour did nothing to lighten Tom's mood, and by the time the message began, he was breathing silent curses under his breath. Even the sermon seemed off key—the evangelist was speaking to teen-agers and Tom could not relate to his words. Ellen did try to follow the sermon, but she was preoccupied by personal troubles.

When the message ended, the Bryants, although there seemed no logical reason for them to do so, rose from their seats and walked hand-in-hand to the area in front of the platform. They were counseled by the pastor of a pentecostal church, and after twenty minutes of conversation, prayer and not a few tears, Tom and Ellen made decisions for Christ. When I asked the young couple what brought them forward, Ellen could only say that they were drawn out of a sense of despondency. Somehow, Ellen said, change appeared possible if they would only reach out to grasp it.

He had a drinking problem

For the last several months Bill Franklin had delivered a considerable amount of mail marked with a "Billy Graham Mississippi Crusade" return address. Bill is a native of a small delta town; he has lived in Jackson most of his adult life and it has been years since he has been in a church. The Billy Graham envelopes piqued his curiosity, and tonight he decided to come out to the meeting.

Franklin is a fifty-three-year-old widower. For the last fifteen years he has been addicted to alcohol, and although he is usually careful enough to limit his serious drinking to weekends, holidays and vacations he occasionally has to take a day or two off from his route to recover from an alcoholic stupor.

He arrived at the meeting early and found a seat in the end-zone stands. Bill liked the singing—it reminded him of the little church he used to attend as a child. He tried to pay careful attention to the sermon, but the rain and chill bothered him a great deal. Toward the end of the message, he heard Graham say how one could be certain of eternal life, and from that point on he followed the evangelist's every word.

When the invitation was given, Franklin was one of the first persons to head for the platform area. He was counseled by the middle-aged proprietor of a hardware store. Bill was very concerned about his drinking problem and wanted to know if what Graham had said about all things becoming new when a man accepted Christ was accurate. The counselor assured him that God would make him into a new man if he believed in Christ. Bill prayed with the merchant, who promised to telephone him the next evening.

Sense of sin

Sarah Herndon came to the stadium after a long and tiring day at the supermarket. During the day she made several incorrect rings on her cash register, and Mr. Johnson, the store manager, kept giving her angry stares. The last few weeks had been very difficult for the eighteen-year-old. Her baby daughter, born out of wedlock three months before, was adopted by a Georgia couple, and Sarah could not get over her sense of desolation and loss.

She had often heard Billy Graham on the radio, and up to eighteen months ago she had been an active church member.

Then she met and fell in love with a Mississippi State University student. They lived together for several months, but when Sarah became pregnant the boy refused to have anything to do with her. Sarah was too ashamed to ask her parents for help, and she took a small room and scraped by on her supermarket job. Her father eventually discovered her condition, placed her under proper medical care and persuaded her to offer the baby up for adoption.

Sarah felt a deep-seated sense of sin, and she came to the meeting hoping to find forgiveness. Yet she remained seated for quite some time after the invitation was initially offered. Then she heard the evangelist say, "There is someone here

who needs to come forward but is holding back. God is talking to you and I want you to come." Sarah felt Graham
knew all about her, and suddenly it was not very difficult to
get out of her seat and move to the infield.

Whites only?

Sometimes all the medical skill and advanced technology
brought to bear in an emergency are not enough to save a
life, and this had been the case today with the heart-attack
victim whose vital signs Linda Mae Rogers had monitored.
After a stable morning, the patient suffered another infarc-
tion and at four-fifteen he died.

Linda, a nurse for fourteen years, was used to death, but
sometimes one worked so hard to pull someone through that
one felt a sense of personal loss when he succumbed. There
was a special kind of poignancy to this death. The victim
was white, he had resided in an all-white neighborhood, and
it was only in the very last hours of his life that he had come
into close contact with a black person.

Linda hadn't planned to go to hear Billy Graham—she
suspected he was really here to talk to white people, but
when her shift ended she decided to grab a quick dinner
and drive over to the stadium. Her husband, Fred, an interstate trucker, was in Memphis on an overnight trip. Linda
came from a nominal religious background—her parents
were members of an AME congregation, but she and Fred
were not really interested in attending church.

When Linda arrived at the stadium and looked around at
the crowd and the choir she was surprised to find a
significant number of blacks present. She wondered if some
of these people had come out of curiosity or because of a
sense of association and belonging. She felt greatly convinced by the sermon, not that she believed herself to be
guilty of any major sin, but what the evangelist said about a
person's need of salvation seemed to make sense, and she
went forward with alacrity when the invitation was made.

When Graham finishes addressing the inquirers, he returns to the trailer. He will relax and wait there until the

crowd has dissipated. Even so, scores of persons will wait near his car in hopes of seeing or talking to him.

Tonight the evangelist's fashionably longish hair needs trimming and he will be visited by a local barber. The barber is brought to the trailer by a Methodist pastor. As the two men enter the room, the clergyman takes Graham aside and says, "This man is under the conviction of the Holy Spirit. I believe he is ready to receive Christ." As the barber deftly moves his comb and scissors, Graham inquires into the man's background. Is he married, how many children does he have? Graham asks the barber if he is a Christian. The man replies that he is not sure, he has never made a definite commitment to Christ. Billy asks if he would now like to do so. "Yes, I want Christ as my Savior."

Graham has a few moments before seen hundreds of people come forward to make a decision for Christ, and this of course is only the very tip of the iceberg of the multitudes of persons who have made this commitment under his preaching. Still he is at root a soul winner—this is his personal raison d'être and he patiently and firmly guides the man to Christ.

CHAPTER 9

THE END OF A
VERY LONG DAY

Graham places a call to the Municipal Airport and he
reaches Johnny Cash as the singer is about to board his private jet for the return trip to Nashville. He thanks Cash and
then says a brief hello to June Carter. Grady comes into the
trailer; it is time to go over to Jim Carr's home.

Billy, Grady and T.W. leave the field and return to the
Holiday Inn to prepare for the dinner party. On the way to
the hotel Billy is disconcerted—he cannot find his large-print
pulpit Bible, and T.W. radios Don Bailey with a request to
look for it on the platform. Don, who is halfway to the Hilton with a carful of staff, continues on to the hotel, drops his
passengers and returns to the stadium. There he encounters
Charlie Riggs standing in the driving rain with a black teen-
ager. The youth has come forward but he feels he will continue facing serious personal problems and he expresses a
desire to talk to Graham. Charlie informs the young man
that Billy has left the area, but he writes down the teen's

name and address and promises to try to set up an appointment.

Riggs and Bailey then begin to search the platform for Graham's Bible. Their efforts are fruitless, and they walk together toward Don's car. As they pass the grandstand a stunned father asks Riggs where he can pick up his lost daughter, and the man is directed to the security office. The two colleagues shake their heads. It has been a long day—perhaps they can enjoy a bit of relaxation and fellowship at the Carrs' home.

When Don reaches his automobile, T.W. is on the radio telling him that Grady has found the missing Bible under the back seat of the Pontiac. The stadium electrician is cutting off the floodlights and the last cars are moving out of the parking lot, but there is still work to be done.

Follow-up

In the nearby Mississippi Armory a crew of two hundred people, known in the terminology of the Graham apparatus as the "co-labor corps," are starting a four-hour shift. These people will initiate the follow-up process, which, if successful, will enable the eight hundred and fifty-two persons who made decisions tonight to grow in their Christian commitment. The co-laborers are seated at several aluminum folding tables. Their work is divided into several segments. Some collate personal information cards completed by the counselors; others make several copies of each card—one remains with the Crusade committee, another is forwarded to the Graham headquarters in Minneapolis, a third copy is mailed immediately to either the inquirer's pastor or to a minister whose congregation is located in the inquirer's neighborhood. The room is noisy, busy and swelteringly hot. Messengers traverse the area picking up finished forms, and a young man who can barely read or write but who wanted to help in the Crusade passes out hamburgers and sodas from a large cardboard box. When the workers are about halfway through their chores, TV star Jerry Clower and Cliff Barrows come by to greet them.

Clower, who had received a standing ovation from his fellow Mississippians the evening before, tells a few stories about the "Hee Haw" show and discusses his career in the entertainment field. "It was a thrill to get back into show business, to make an album, and eight months later it sold a million dollars' worth. It was a thrill that every album I have ever made has been a national hit. It was a thrill to me to be inducted into the world-famous Grand Old Opry and it was a thrill to be in the new Roy Rogers movie. I am not going to stand here and tell you that I'm not human enough to have been thrilled. But I want to go on record to say the greatest thrill I have ever had is when I was saved at Liberty, Mississippi. The preacher got up and said, 'For all have sinned and come short of the glory of God.' I said, 'He ain't talking about everybody.' And then the preacher said, 'For the wages of sin is death.' I said, 'My goodness. He means me,' and I accepted Christ."

Each night Team members and special guests visit the colaborers, and there is usually much good-natured kidding. The evening before Grady told of the time he and Billy were received by the Archbishop of Canterbury. The prelate, who was not terribly enamored of American evangelists, asked how Graham and his party traveled to Great Britain. Billy answered that they came on the *Queen Elizabeth*. The Archbishop stiffly replied, "Well, you know our Lord entered Jerusalem on a donkey." Grady cried out, "Well, my Lord Archbishop, if you can tell me how to cross the Atlantic on an ass I'll be glad to do so."

High-court judge sorts cards

At one of the tables near the back of the armory I notice a pleasant-looking couple intently studying a batch of green cards. I walk over and am introduced to Judge and Mrs. Robert P. Sugg. Mr. Sugg is an associate justice of the Mississippi Supreme Court. The judge has taken some vacation time to help in the Crusade, and he and Mrs. Sugg are very delighted to be involved in the co-labor effort.

I ask if sorting cards and checking addresses is not terribly dull for an official of the state's highest judicial body, but Sugg replies, "I wouldn't miss it for anything in the world. This is a marvelous opportunity to participate in a great effort. I am the recipient of many blessings."

The Suggs were recruited by their pastor, and Mrs. Sugg conducted a home prayer group. She is also a counselor, and one evening she talked with a black girl of fourteen who said, "I've been praying since I was ten for Billy Graham to come to Mississippi, and I'm so excited I don't know what to do."

The judge takes considerable pride in the locale of the Crusade. "As I have sat hearing Dr. Graham saying we are in Mississippi Memorial Stadium I have been thrilled to realize that people around the world would know that he was in our state."

All reportorial objectivity aside, I am impressed by the sight of a high-court judge sitting in a dank, humid room until 2 A.M. thumbing through a copy of the Jackson telephone directory. I have to believe this kind of concern and dedication is directly related to Graham, even though the Suggs have never met the evangelist and I would guess that none of the persons in the armory have ever spent any time with Graham. Yet they trust, respect and feel genuine affection for the man.

Judge Sugg tells me, "We don't know Billy Graham personally, but we know he is a tremendous influence for the witness of Christ, and we are very thankful for him."

Out of the mouth of babes

I leave the co-laborers and quickly make my way to the quiet northeast Jackson residential area where Jim Carr lives. As I enter the comfortable one-story, four-bedroom home, I hear the sounds people make when they are relaxed and comfortable with each other.

There are about forty visitors in the Carr house—Billy, Grady, T.W., Walter Smyth, Bev Shea and several other Team members have joined a few close friends of the Carrs' and a number of key Crusade officials. In addition, Graham asked the Carrs to invite six to eight people including the editor of the *Baptist Record*, the executive secretary of the State Baptist Convention and a few leaders of the 1952 Jackson Crusade.

Actually Graham's acceptance of the Carrs' invitation marks a break with his usual practice; normally he will not attend any strictly social functions during a Crusade. Martha Carr, however, has been pleasantly persistent in asking the evangelist to her home, and the Graham people feel genuine affection for Jim, who has labored so long and hard to bring their organization to Jackson.

This is a stand-up affair—a buffet table with hot chili, sandwiches and salad has been laid out, and the guests circulate between the den, playroom and dining area.

When he has finished eating, Graham relaxes in a brown recliner and Dickie, the Carrs' six-year-old, climbs up in the evangelist's lap. The child points his finger at Graham and says, "I know you're a preacher, you jabber, jabber all the time."

This cracks Billy up. In an instant all of the strain and pressure and awesome responsibilities he has experienced and encountered during this long and exhausting day disappear, and someone on the other side of the room whispers, "Out of the mouth of babes."

Coffee is served, then Governor Waller comes in from a late meeting at the Capitol. He and Graham warmly greet each other. Some people talk about the evening's service, most marvel at the patience and fortitude of the crowd in the face of the heavy rain. Soon it is time to leave, tomorrow with all its burdens and opportunities is almost here. Graham and his associates make their departure, and as Billy goes out the front door he lifts Dickie up and the boy smiles happily and says, "Dr. Graham, you and me are buddies."

The other guests make their exit, and Carr remembers an

earlier conversation when Martha said to him, "James I've been so impressed with everybody I've met in the organization. I just hope when I meet Dr. Graham I won't be disappointed," and Jim knows that Martha has not been disappointed in the slightest.

On the way back to the Holiday Inn, Billy, Grady and T.W. quietly discuss the service. Grady reminds them of the rainy night during the first Jackson Crusade when R. G. LeTourneau, a businessman and staunch supporter of their work, was speaking on "power." His talk was interrupted by a bolt of lightning which knocked out the stadium's electrical system and sent a severe shock through his body.

"I want power," LeTourneau quickly said, "but not that kind of power."

It is eleven fifty-five when the car pulls into the hotel driveway. Grady drops Billy and T.W. off. He must continue on to the Hilton to arrange for an early breakfast meeting with some of the association's board members. The lobby is empty and the two old friends easily make their way to the elevator. The men go to their rooms. This will be one more night of a lifetime of evenings spent in similar settings, many miles from home and family.

After sixteen hours, to rest

Outside the rain has ended, a half moon climbs out of the clouds in the western sky, tomorrow promises to be fair. For the last sixteen hours, the evangelist has been surrounded by people. Now he is alone and although he could still, at this late hour, communicate with millions of persons simply by lifting the telephone and dialing a news service, he will not do so—he relishes this time of privacy.

For the next seven hours his fame and renown will not matter, he will be just a man, albeit one of unusual gifts and attainments, who tries, like all other men, to get through the night as best he can. When he looks in the mirror he will not see a face immediately recognized by many of the world's citizens; rather he will wonder if the man whose reflection

confronts him has done all he could for the cause that moti-
vates and shapes his life and has brought him to this place.

And because of the kind of man he is, Billy Graham will
not pause to consider what his coming to Jackson has accomplished, nor will he ponder the tremendous impact he
has had upon the city: how lives have been changed, how
people who once regarded each other as strangers have
begun to develop a sense of community, how blacks and
whites in this traditional seat of racial animosity have for
the first time visited each other's neighborhoods, churches
and homes.

Instead he will think of the persons who did not come forward tonight, of the refugees in distress on Guam, of the
hundreds of people who have tried to reach him today, of
the masses who will eventually view the telecast of this evening's service, of the meetings scheduled later this year in
Europe, Texas and the Far East. And he will think also of his
close friends, of Ruth and his children, and he will be assured, as he is every night of his life, that the God who
brought him to the tent outside Charlotte and who has sent
him across the nation and the world to preach his word will
continue to guide and bless him. And this uniquely authen-
tic man will be satisfied and he will rest—and tomorrow he
will continue running the race.